Sunk By
The *BISMARCK*

The Life and Death
of the
Battleship HMS *Hood*

Edwin P. Hoyt

STEIN AND DAY/*Publishers*/New York

First published in the United States of America in 1980

Copyright © 1977 by Edwin P. Hoyt

All rights reserved

Printed in the United States of America

Stein and Day/*Publishers*/Scarborough House

Briarcliff Manor, New York 10510

Library of Congress Cataloging in Publication Data

Hoyt, Edwin Palmer.
    Sunk by the Bismarck.

    Reprint of the ed. published by Barker, London
under title: The life and death of HMS Hood.
    Bibliography: p.
    Includes index.
    1. Hood (Battle cruiser) I. Title.
VA458.H6H69 1980   359.3'253'0941   80-5401
ISBN 0-8128-2730-9

Contents

Illustrations

The third *Hood* in 1893 (*Imperial War Museum*)
HMS *Hood* at the turn of the century (*Imperial War Museum*)
The last *Hood* at anchor in 1933 (*Imperial War Museum*)
Two amidships details (*Imperial War Museum*)
The launching of SMS *Bismarck* (*Keystone Press Agency*)
SMS *Bismarck* at sea (*Keystone Press Agency*)
The *Bismarck*'s guns (*Keystone Press Agency*)
Prince of Wales (*Keystone Press Agency*)
Prinz Eugen in Boston (*Keystone Press Agency*)

I

The Ship

She was born in the heat of the European war that began in the autumn of 1914, created in the critical days of 1915 when naval intelligence learned that the Kaiser's navy was building several battle-cruisers to be armed with 15-inch guns.

Out of the confusion and the planning of the naval constructors, came a number of designs for big fighting ships. They all considered the problems of armament to withstand both the bigger guns that seemed to be in the offing and naval torpedoes.

When these were submitted to the Board of the Admiralty, the matter of sorting them out took a bit of time. Then there were no large berths available in the shipyards for the construction of so large a craft. One delay led to another, and orders were held up all during the terrible winter of 1915–16.

It was March when the chosen design was finally given the stamp of approval, and all the red tape cleared away. Chief Constructor E. L. Attwood could then heave a mighty sigh of relief and get on with the job at hand. He had conceived a stately and gallant fighting ship that would be the finest Britain could produce. She was to have sleek, low lines that bespoke enormous power in the best of Britain's naval tradition.

She was to be 860 feet long, and more than a hundred feet in the beam. She was to displace 36,000 tons, to carry eight 15-inch guns, sixteen 5·5-inch guns, and two 21-inch torpedo tubes. As for armour, she was to be the equal of *Tiger*, with an 8-inch belt of armour plating around her, and 9-inch barbettes, to protect the turrets She was to make thirty-two knots, which would make her one of the fastest ships afloat.

In April orders were placed for four ships. *Anson* was to be built at Armstrongs, *Howe* at Cammell Laird, *Rodney* at Fairfields, and the ship that would be known to the public as the Mighty *Hood* was to be laid down at John Brown's yard.

Scarcely had the templates been put into order when June brought the reports of Jutland's fierce fight. The Admiralty began to worry about the protection of these mighty ships in a modern world. So the idea that Admiral Fisher had propounded with such success in the creation of the battle-cruisers – that speed is its own best guarantee of safety – was questioned, turned over, and finally rejected in the case of these mighty vessels. Speed was not enough, the Board decided, and the plans for *Hood* must be changed quite radically to make her conform to the new ideas.

Anyone who has ever designed a ship would realize what this entailed. It was not simply a matter of rationalizing all the changed dimensions, it was a question of rethinking whole concepts of design. And so the idea developed. The Fisher plan for a battle-cruiser with armour on the second-class scale was thrown out. This ship was intended for the battle line, so that it had to be tough enough to take the worst the potential enemy could deal out. She was in other words to become a super warship.

In the redrafting, the protection demanded by the Admiralty was to be accomplished by making her deeper. There would have to be some slight loss in speed but that could not be helped. It was always a trade-off – and the Admiralty had decided after the inconclusive Jutland battle that protection was more important than speed.

So the armour-belt was increased from 8 inches to a full foot in thickness. Twelve inches of solid steel ought to stop the heaviest projectile known to the world, send it bouncing off harmlessly into the water, or at very worst, contain its head and its explosive power within the belt and keep it out of the vitals of the battleship. The barbettes were also made 12 inches thick, and would assure the total protection of the men who manned the ship's big guns.

In the region of the magazines, there was also to be much more protection than had been anticipated for the battle-cruiser design. Since the magazines were forward and aft, directly beneath the big guns, they had the protection of the armour belting and the barbettes to begin with. The deck plating was thickened here, and since there were several decks to protect the magazines, the design seemed sensible and the safety factors carefully considered.

As these changes were being made, so were others. The gun elevation was raised to a full 30° which gave her additional range. The torpedo equipment was made more modern, based on other lessons learned at Jutland and after. Anti-flash precautions were taken to be sure that the magazines did not suffer from the manning of the ship's own guns.

When all this was worked out, it added an additional 5,000 tons to the big ship's displacement, and brought her well up over the 40,000-ton mark.

Of course all the problems of metacentric height and stability were worked out time and again to make sure no errors had crept in. It was not impossible for such changes to create a ship that might turn turtle and embarrass an entire naval establishment. But that was certainly not the case in the care lavished on *Hood* as she was being built.

Meanwhile work on other ships of this design had not really progressed far. For in the diminishing ability of Germany to carry on the sea war, and the general knowledge that the British fleet controlled the surface of the sea, the Kaiser's Imperial Navy had stopped construction on its big ships *Graf Spee*, *Prinz Eitel Friedrich* and *Furst Bismarck*.

At the Admiralty it was recalled that the purpose of the big ships then under construction was to offset that German threat. The construction of *Howe*, *Anson* and *Rodney* was halted in 1917. Some £860,000 had been spent on these massive ships, but it was deemed best not to throw good money after what might be bad, or at least make more unnecessary expenditure in a rapidly changing naval world.

Hood had been laid down in September 1916, and the work had progressed nicely. Furthermore, she represented something so radical in design and concept that support for her from Whitehall was strong, and so the construction continued. She was launched in late August of 1918, and even though the armistice came less than three months later, the decision was made to complete her. By this time she had an additional four 4-inch anti-aircraft guns, and four 3-pounders, and four more torpedo tubes. She was a floating fortress, and the concept of her might awed those who came to see her as the fitting out began.

The workmen swarmed over the ship, tens, dozens, scores, hundreds of them, little ants with their welding rods and riveting tools, their hammers and wedges and pliers. Already, of course, in the pubs and the village squares she was coming to be known as 'the Mighty 'Ood'. Even though the war had been won, Britain knew that the fleet must be maintained.

When she was completed in the spring of 1920, the public soon learned that she had cost more than £6m! But who cared? For was she not the greatest warship afloat in the world? She was the largest, the fastest and the finest. She was and she would be for twenty years the queen battleship of the world. That is why she had a special place in the history of Britain's sea power that could be matched by no other vessel.

She had her difficulties, most of them the result of re-designing in midstream. She drew three feet more than originally intended because of that extra armour, and she had a reduced freeboard because of it. To an extent this was offset by an unusual sheer at bow and stern, but still, in a sea-way the quarterdeck flooded, which could be most inconvenient for all concerned on a chilly day.

The clever construction of her hull gave maximum pro-tection through armour, with the minimum of armour to do it. Thus she had protection where it counted, and if some compartments were to flood, they would not hurt much by doing so.

The designers and the builders suggested that she could stand the force of several torpedoes without even slowing down. It seemed inconceivable that a u-boat or any other submarine could ever sink her.

As for aerial bombardment, her decks and plating were such as to withstand the shock of virtually anything the planes could drop, at least as known in 1920. She had also been specifically designed to withstand shellfire from opposing capital ships. Thats what all the armour plating was really about.

So she was there, queen of the seas, considered more powerful than the *Queen Elizabeth*, with extra deck armour and thinner plating where thick plating seemed unnecessary. Decks and turret tops, of course, were not considered need-ful of protection.

Her power plant was as efficient as anything about her with geared turbines that the engineers declared to be the greatest afloat. She had three engine rooms and she had made 32·07 knots on her trials. With a heavy load of 44,000 tons, she could make nearly 32 knots.

As for the accommodation for captain, officers, and men, this was nothing short of luxurious compared with that on earlier vessels. Special attention had been drawn by the designers to the need for better ventilation in such a large ship. She would, after all, carry a crew larger than many a village, and with some 1,400 men cramped together even on a ship her size, there could be no limit to the breathing room. So the ventilating fans were many and accommodation was large and spacious throughout the vessel.

When *Hood* was commissioned, she was given into the care of Captain W. Tomkinson, one of the most deserving captains in the Royal Navy. In the spring he brought together officers and men, and began the further trials that would make a fighting unit of her.

Of course no one expected to be doing any fighting these days. The war had just ended and peace not yet really secured. The state of the world could be best described as one of numb shock, with hope shining more brightly than a June sun in London.

The Royal Navy fitted her ships and then fitted her crews to fight those ships. Lucky was the man, as all England knew, who served in the Royal Navy and found himself a berth aboard this empress of the fleet.

In May Captain Tomkinson learned he would take her with *Tiger* and nine destroyers on a summer cruise to the Scandinavian countries.

First, however, she must show herself to those in authority. On 18 May her crewmen on the quarter-deck hoisted the flag of Rear-Admiral Sir Roger B. Keyes, commander of the battle-cruiser squadron of the Atlantic Fleet at Cawsand Bay. Next day she sailed for Plymouth Sound, and there she moved in alongside nos 6 and 7 wharves.

For the next few days there was leave for nearly all hands as she was already provisioned. The men who stayed aboard mended clothes and did light duty. Those ashore were already establishing the legend in the pubs where sailors went to drink. They found eager ears, because who in all England did not revere the fleet, and who did not have that little bit of envy for the brave sailors who challenged the sea in both war and peace?

After a week, she went on torpedo trials, and all seemed to work well, except that towards the end one torpedo failed to run. Now why was that? The Admiralty would certainly want to know. Divers were sent for and they came alongside, went down, checked the tubes, and made some little adjustments. Next day she was out again and the trials were much more satisfactory. The torpedoes ran and the ship performed as nicely as anyone could expect. She was indeed a beauty, and a proud one.

On 29 May she was at sea again, simulating a fierce struggle with the fleet's own submarines. She would have to be ready for that, for the possible tracking and hunting by an enemy. This day she proved she was. The admiral, the captain, the senior officers and above all Whitehall were distinctly pleased with the performance of the new queen of Britain's battleships.

2

The Tradition

The very name of *Hood* is hallowed in British naval history, for its bearers, human and ship, carried on their brave endeavours in the grand period of Britain's naval might.

The first naval Hood was Samuel Hood, son of the vicar of Thorncombe in Dorset, who was born in 1724. When young Hood was sixteen years old he joined the Navy as a midshipman. Six years later, in 1746, he was promoted to lieutenant, a sign of the high esteem in which he was held and the excellence of his service, for a vicar's son had little influence in naval circles.

Some men lived out their lives as lieutenants, then were put ashore on half pay or even none at all, and expected to grub for livings as if they had never been to sea at all. Lieutenant Samuel Hood was luckier than that, however, and when he was thirty years old he was promoted to commander.

That was not the most brilliant of careers, of course, but it was serviceable. Two years later he was fortunate to be made a post-captain, which, at thirty-two, was a considerable achievement. Then he served on the various stations that demanded naval attention in that day, the western Atlantic, the Caribbean, and the glorious Mediterranean. He distinguished himself.

The real time for glory was yet to come. Come it did when the perennial wars against France were complicated by the insurrection of the North American colonies, or what those on the western shore of the Atlantic call the American Revolution.

Captain Hood spent much of that war on the West Indian station, where the American privateers came to prey, and where the American blockade runners came for sugar and rum and any other supplies they might find to assist the beleaguered colonies.

So distinguished was his conduct, so excellent the reports on him, and so grateful his monarch, that he was made Admiral of the Blue Squadron in 1780 and commander of the West Indies station.

He was at Dominica in 1782 and shared in the grand victory there, flying his flag in *Barfleur*, and capturing four ships before he took the surrender of the French *Ville de Paris*. For this he was honoured by King George with a peerage. He became Baron Hood of Catherington in Ireland.

The course was then ever upward. Lord Hood became a Lord of the Admiralty in 1788, a post he held until the French Revolution, when in 1793 he became commander of the Mediterranean station. There was indeed both honour and challenge, for he was to direct the occupation of the French naval fort of Toulon, and the vital operations in the Gulf of Lyons and off the coast of Corsica.

The distinguished career was unmarred. He served until 1795, when he hauled down his flag for the last time, and retired with his memories to Bath. A grateful sovereign created him Viscount Hood of Whitley, and he lived a happy, gouty old age, dying at Bath on 27 June 1816 at the age of ninety-two.

Samuel's brother, Alexander, who was two years younger, joined the service at the same time, and was promoted lieutenant in the same year. It took him two years longer, however, until 1756, to reach the rank of commander. His career then took a distinctly upward turn, and he was made Flag-Captain to Admiral Charles Saunders in the Mediterranean station. He was given command of the *Minerva*, and took her into Quiberon Bay to fight in the victorious battle there under Admiral Lord Hawke. Then it was on to the Bay of Biscay, where he ran across the *Warwick*, an unfortunate ship that had been captured by the wily French several years before. Young Captain Hood distinguished himself when he cut her out and took her after a bloody battle lasting six hours.

He was indeed a fighting captain. His service was even more distinguished by gallantry than his brother's. So it was not seen amiss that, when in 1780 the elder Hood was made Admiral of the Blue Squadron, the younger became on the same day Rear-Admiral of the White Squadron. Young Hood had been commander of the yacht *Katherine* and Treasurer of Greenwich Hospital, so that he had shown his administrative ability as well as his valour.

Soon enough, the Admiral of the White Squadron was out fighting again in those endless wars against the French, and under him, flying his flag was *Queen*, a ship of the line with 90 guns. He was serving then under Admiral Lord Howe and was engaged in the relief of Gibraltar in 1782.

Five years later, while his brother was on the West Indian station, Alexander was promoted Vice-Admiral. Six years after that he was second-in-command to Lord Howe, with his flag in *Royal George*.

His valour in the Battle of The Glorious First of June earned him a barony. He became Baron Bridport. In 1795 he was back at sea fighting the French off Lorient and taking three of their ships. This action brought him command of the Channel Fleet, a post he held until he hauled down his flag in 1800. He, too, was promoted in civil rank again, to be a Viscount, and he, too, lived to a ripe and happy old age, dying two years before his brother.

The story of the Hoods is complicated, as is so often the case with distinguished families, by the emergence of another branch in the higher reaches of the Navy. This

branch had two sons, also named Alexander and Samuel.
The second Alexander joined Rodney as a midshipman in
1767 while his younger brother Samuel came along nine
years later.

Alexander served as a midshipman under his already
distinguished cousin, Captain Samuel. He was then offered
one of the grand sailing opportunities of all time, he was
chosen to join Captain Cook on his second voyage around
the world. His promotion followed rapidly, becoming a
lieutenant in 1777 and a commander four years later. He
once more served with his cousin, Sir Samuel now, as
flag-captain on the West Indian station. He was along at
Dominica in the *Champion*.

His career progressed rapidly. He had several ships in the
war against France and was particularly distinguished in his
service with the Channel Fleet. In 1797 he was given the
74-gun ship *Mars* and soon took her into action. Next year
he engaged the French ship *Hercule* in a desperate struggle in
which he was killed in action, just before the Frenchman
surrendered.

Finally his brother Samuel lived a life as respected and
valiant as had his relatives. Coming into the navy just at
the time of the American troubles, he was lucky in that, with
the increased demands upon the Royal Navy, promotions
were easier and life was more exciting than it had ever been in
the past.

He joined *Courageux*, commanded by Cousin Samuel, and
in five years he was a lieutenant. In 1782 he was given a
lieutenant's dream, a ship of his own, the sloop *Renard*. He
sailed her in the West Indies looking for Frenchmen and for
rebels.

Soon he was a post captain, and in 1791 he had *Juno*, a
frigate of 32 guns. He distinguished himself as much by
his compassion as his gallantry. In that same year he was
given a sword called the 100 guinea sword by the House of

Assembly in Jamaica. The reward was for rescuing three stranded seamen from a wreck during a storm.

In the Mediterranean in 1793, he narrowly escaped capture when he entered Toulon one night not knowing that the English fleet had just left, and that the port was back in the hands of the French. He had anchored and his ship was then fired upon by the shore batteries. She was very nearly sunk, but he escaped by cutting the cable and sailing out.

In 1796 he was at the battle of the Nile, in command of *Zealous*. He captured *Le Guerrier* after a few minutes of action, and so well did he distinguish himself that when the battle was ended, Lord Nelson left him as senior officer of the squadron blockading Napoleon's army in Egypt. He did his work well, and his ships captured thirty French troop transports.

At Algeciras in 1801 he commanded *Venerable*, and a year later he was back in the West Indies as commodore with his pennant in *Centaur*. He brought a ship into the Royal Navy, commissioning the *Diamond Rock*, a privateer off Martinique which he armed with 24- and 18-pound guns to go out and fight the French.

In 1803 he took the Dutch West Indian settlements of Demerara, Berbice and Essequibo. His action in the war continued until 1805 by which time he was in command of the British squadron that met the French off Rochefort. In this action, in *Centaur*, he was wounded and the surgeons had to cut off his right arm.

In 1807, he was promoted Rear-Admiral. He fought in the Baltic in 1808, flying his flag in *Implacable*. He fought the Russians and took the ship of the line *Sewolod*, a feat which won him much honour. He was made baronet in 1809, a vice-admiral in 1811, and commander-in-chief of the East Indies fleet in 1811.

He went to the East, and there he died of a fever on Christmas Eve, 1814.

Such a distinguished line of British seamen demanded recognition from the nation. It came in the course of the years with the creation of several ships of the name Hood.

The first of these was named after Admiral Hood of the Blue Squadron. She was commissioned in his honour just two years after he had hauled down his flag and retired to Bath. She was not much of a vessel to be sure. A hired ship of 14 guns engaged in convoy duties in the North Sea during the war, she did not even last long. She was restored to her owners and her original name in 1798.

But the tradition had been established. HMS *Lord Hood* had existed, and it was a fine name and an honourable one for a ship.

The second *Hood* was a second-rate sailing ship of 80 guns launched in 1859. She sailed for many years, and then was bastardized by conversion to steam and made a screw line battleship of 91 guns. She was a miserable specimen and had a miserable life, quite out of character for Hood. She ended her days as a barracks ship for the Royal Engineers submarine miners at Chatham, and was sold out of the navy in 1888.

The third *Hood* had a much more glamorous career as was fitting. She was launched in July of 1891 as a twin-screw battleship of 14 guns, with a speed of 17·5 knots and a displacement of 14,000 tons. She joined the Mediterranean squadron and assisted in the pacification of Crete in 1896. She then lived a quiescent life for some years, but in 1914 went out gallantly. She was sunk at the entrance to Portland harbour as a block-ship against German u-boats that had been firing torpedoes through the southern entrance to the harbour.

This then was the background and the heritage of the gallant ship named *Hood* that joined the Home Fleet in the summer of 1920.

3

Happy Time

When Rear-Admiral Sir Roger B. Keyes hoisted his flag in HMS *Hood* and the press reported that the pride of the fleet was heading for Scandinavia, all Britain was cheered. The Admiral was going to show the flag and indicate to their northern friends that Britain had come out of the war with her naval reputation undiminished.

After an uneventful voyage across the North Sea *Hood*, *Tiger* and nine destroyers arrived at Kioge Bay. The French were already inside, but that made no difference. When the mighty *Hood* appeared, she stole the show from all the warships in the area.

It was a busy time. The King's birthday was 3 June, so that the evening of the second was spent dressing the ship and putting the men's clothing and belongings in order. Next day she was as clean and shining as she had ever been, and the men formed on deck to give three cheers for His Majesty. Captain Tomkinson was a proud man that day.

It had been anticipated that the British flotilla visiting Sweden would go to Stockholm, but not this year, for *Hood*'s draught was too great for the harbour there. Instead, she stayed on the outer edges, in good deep battleship water for the festivities that marked the summer cruises.

On 4 June she was at Kalmar with Swedish planes flying around the squadron in salute. She, in turn, unlimbered those great guns, to give a 21–gun salute to the Swedish admiral who was the senior officer of his country in attendance.

Next day the British consul arrived on board and received

the 7-gun salute that was accorded to his rank. On 6 June the guns celebrated with 21 shots the name day of the Swedish king. The ship was dressed in flags and bunting, the atmosphere was distinctly carnival.

It continued in that manner. On 7 June the Swedish ships' guns saluted for half an hour, the harbour smelled of cordite and smoke wreathed the sky above the fleets.

Three days later Captain Tomkinson conned the flagship to Nyna-Shamn, and there the King of Sweden came to visit *Hood*, since *Hood* could not come to Stockholm to visit him. He brought along the Crown Prince, and together they spent two hours on board, joining the captain and his officers in the wardroom for a reception. The crew manned the sides and cheered them. They also cheered the British minister when he got his 17-gun salute.

Of course, the proceedings were all reported back home in the papers, and in the pubs at night the regulars stopped for a moment over their pints and talked about the marvellous 'do' going on across the North Sea.

There was, of course, some touch of reality involved in the summer cruise. On 13 June the squadron was at sea and the Admiral called for exercises that included experiments in making smoke. *Hood* and *Tiger* blew smoke at each other all afternoon and the destroyers screened one, and then the other, to test their power to protect the big ships in an attack situation.

They came to Apenrade, and here the festivities were interrupted rudely for those who were put to work scraping and painting. New as she was, *Hood* was still a man-made creature on the sea, and she was subject to that old devil rust which must be kept at arm's length in peace and in war.

There was a spot of tragedy, too, when on 15 June Chief Stoker Petty Officer Sidney Hingston died of pneumonia. Had it happened at sea, he might have been buried a sailor's way, but it had happened on a cruise and in harbour, and so the decision was made that he be shipped home to England for burial on land. With ceremony, the body was moved ashore for shipment home.

The sadness subsided soon enough. There was too much to do. There were the daily chores of seamanship and the special jobs of sea-going diplomacy. The Royal Marines held infantry drill the morning after Chief Hingston had gone away, and by midday it was as if he had never been among them. Small wonder, for were there not nearly 1,500 men aboard this fighting town?

Hood hoisted in her anchors, and sailed for Copenhagen on 18 June. On arrival there were the usual salutes and ceremonies, involving also the Germans this time, which was rather uncomfortable for some of the officers and other ranks who found it hard to erase their memories of the last war. But they were, after all, the guests of the King of Denmark, that close cousin of the Germans, and so all concerned swallowed whatever emotions troubled them and they made their salutes and sallies with a will.

Hood was the talk of the court, the talk of Denmark's sailing men, the talk of every place she showed that proud cutwater. The King of Denmark came to see her, and insisted on bringing his Queen and the whole royal retinue. It was not often that he had such a chance, nor that such a behemoth of the seas showed her face. They spent a pleasant two hours aboard, while the Admiral and Captain Tomkinson explained the wonders of the vessel to them.

Next day officers of the Royal Danish Navy showed up and it had to be done all over again by the captain and his senior officers. The following day, the anniversary of His Majesty's coronation, was another ship's holiday. There were salutes and parades and all kinds of festivities in the messes. Throughout all this the men still worked the ship and kept her sound and ready for sea.

On 24 June they headed for Christiania and another round of entertainments and mutual attempts to impress.

Life aboard the ship was easy – in terms of naval discipline of course. On Sundays the Roman Catholics went to *Tiger* for mass, and the Anglicans stayed aboard the *Hood*. The Presbyterians and the others sometimes had hard lines of it, but usually attempts were made to care for the religious needs of every man aboard.

There was leave, and there was a certain amount of drunkenness and misbehaviour. There was, between times of celebrating, plenty of work for those who liked it. On 2 July they were back on station in Scapa Flow, getting ready for power trials with the squadron. They would also go out for firing practice.

The plan was nearly scotched by a thick sheet of fog that rolled in that day, but the Admiral was not to be denied and *Hood* went out to do her work. The manoeuvres called for her to be a target for the submarines; the Navy was testing its supership and its fighting submariners at the same time. She had her screen, and they travelled at about 15 knots, for these were exercises after all.

On 3 July the trials continued, and in the submarine exercises, *Hood* was 'hit' by a torpedo. But, of course, she was supposedly not even to be slowed by a single hit, so that no one worried much about that; instead there were drinks in the wardroom of the lucky submarine and nearly everyone was pleased.

Late that afternoon of 3 July, *Hood* was back in haven at Scapa Flow, anchored in twenty fathoms, swinging gently and gracefully at her cable. There were more exercises. On 4 July she set off for Cromarty, and then for Rosyth, and then there was another task that took some of the bad taste out of the mouths of those who had seen the Germans on the Scandinavian tour. *Hood* was to lead the convoy of ex-German naval capital ships which would be brought out from across the North Sea.

She sent navigators to those ships at Heligoland and

Wesfalen. Marines and sailors searched the vessels for contraband and explosives – no one knew what the former enemy might do, even now.

That exercise in captured hardware involved *Hood* for nearly all of August, and so it was the last day of the month before she returned home, this time to Penzance. She was in and out of port for a few days. On 8 September she was taking on ammunition and supplies at Plymouth, and she then transferred the flag of Rear-Admiral, Battle-Cruiser Squadron to *Glorious*, and took on the flag of Admiral Sir Miles Browning.

That autumn of 1920, *Hood* spent close around England's shores; at Portland for a time, and then at sea undertaking more exercises and fleet drills. After all, she was just working up. It took months and eons of effort to make a fighting unit of a ship and crew, and while no one in the world expected there to be any reason for fighting these days, the Royal Navy had its standards. *Hood* was to bear them proudly.

The ship was a happy ship, but not a loose one. The captain had occasionally to punish offenders, and those included officers as well as men; overspending in the wine department was not an uncommon offence by certain junior officers. Both the first lieutenant and the captain kept an eagle eye out for this offence; many a naval career had wilted in the bud over no more than that.

There were triumphs and there were tragedies. The submarine *R-4* collided with *Tiger* on exercises, which was a tragedy and led to a court martial aboard. By and large, however, these were minor incidents in a placid life, a workmanlike existence carried on by the great warship that moved so calmly through Albion's waters.

Early in 1921 *Hood*, *Repulse* and *Queen Elizabeth* – a mighty trio that – led other ships of His Majesty's Navy out into exercises in Spanish waters. And why not? It was proper to show the flag, and was not the Mediterranean a British lake? The exercises were held in Arosa bay, and on 23 January *Hood* staged special ceremonies for the King of Spain to show the friendship of the Empire.

At the end of the month they were in Vigo, and some of the naval men had their first glimpses of *senoritas* and the beauty of hard, dusty Spain. Then it was off to the Rock, to old Gibraltar, to make a showing, to exhibit *Hood* to some who had not yet seen her in the fleet, and to engage in exercises in this altogether different milieu of the Mediterranean. So there were attacks and exercises, imaginative battles and attacks and the repelling of submarines.

That spring Captain G. Mackworth replaced Tomkinson as commander of the mighty ship. Sadly, for it was always so with a great ship, Tomkinson was piped over the side and went away to do his duty elsewhere.

Had he been an easy-going commander? Some seemed to think so, and if that had been the case, and they expected the same of the new leader, the officers and men were in for a rude surprise. For it was only a matter of days after taking over that Captain Mackworth had begun to look into various matters. The first man to get into serious trouble was one of the paymaster lieutenants, who had been for some time charging wines both to the gunroom and the wardroom simultaneously. An end was put to that practice, but not before the miscreant had made a false statement to the captain, had been discovered and hauled up. For all practical purposes an end had been put to one career.

With that, it was apparent that a new era was in store for the officers and men of *Hood*.

4

Tartars and Targets

Captain Mackworth was a tartar and there was no doubt about it on any deck once he had been aboard for forty-eight hours. One could not say that he ruined the Mediterranean cruise for anyone, but every man was soon on his toes, and every officer made sure of his buttons and his brass. There would be no shirking on *Hood* while this captain was aboard.

In May the ship was back at Devonport changing personnel, taking on supplies, doing a thousand different things that were a part of the peacetime naval routine.

The captain decided that spring that *Hood* was growing tatty, so that the painting and refurbishing took on a faster pace. Three new midshipmen were brought aboard that month and were quickly indoctrinated in their duties and the conduct that the captain expected of them.

The captain was a stickler. One day when an officer of the deck had allowed a smaller vessel to come close alongside the *Hood* when she was moored at Weymouth, the captain grew furious. He tore the officer off a strip, and then inserted a note in the log of the day about the misdemeanour. It was, he said, 'against the spirit of the orders of the captain'. That, of course, was an indefinable crime, but it could hurt a junior officer's chance of promotion.

Hood was a busy ship that summer. She was out with the fleet, conducting exercises, keeping fit and doing the work of the peacetime navy. But she was hardly a happy ship under this strait-laced captain. King George came to visit her at Torbay and the officers and other ranks rallied round to put on the best face they could for the king.

There were incidents – almost insubordination at times – as the day when a lieutenant-commander, who was also holder of the Distinguished Service Cross for valour in the war, was dressed down by the captain, who then in a rage ordered the officer from his cabin. The lieutenant-commander did not leave, and he was 'corrected' – the proceedings noted in the day's log.

In August the ship was in Gibraltar, and the captain was scathing Lieutenant Francis Babington Proudfoot. Proudfoot's crime? As officer of the watch he had shown too much compassion, and failed to arrest a stoker who came back to the ship drunk – as a thousand, and perhaps a thousand thousand stokers had come back to ships drunk before over the years.

The next day the captain rated all his officers for laxity of duty. The following day he was after the petty officers, and the day after that he ordered close-order drills in full uniform in the heat of the Gibraltar summer. He gave his officers and petty officers lectures on their conduct and responsibilities to the ship, to the Navy and to him.

The tension was broken only by Whitehall. One would like to believe the authorities knew of what was happening on *Hood*, and took action to avoid trouble. But quite probably the reason *Hood* was sent out on a mission – to Rio de Janeiro, together with *Repulse* – was that they represented the finest of the fleet. They were to represent king and country at the centenary celebration of Brazilian independence.

The captain never let up. *Hood* did herself proud. At Rio the naval powers assembled, and staged contests in the fashion of time immemorial. Britain defeated the US Navy's best in four of seven boxing bouts. Five of the champions were members of *Hood*'s company.

B

Such victory, however, did not save the men from the captain's almost constant wrath. Day after day names went down in the log, for one petty infraction or another, matters that a better captain would have settled with a word or a transfer. Even the chief surgeon got it one day in Rio for some indefinable crime that the captain saw.

They went then to the West Indies, and still the captain never unbent one inch. Gunner James F. Widgen was rated for letting some of his men drink too much while they were on leave in St Lucia. That is the way it went, all through the western hemisphere, until late November when the ship returned to Gibraltar. The 'old man' seemed to grow worse with the months, not better. One November day a pair of lieutenants were reprimanded for having the temerity to go into the wardroom for a cup of tea when they had the watch. The fact that the ship was in port and at her mooring made not the slightest bit of difference.

Ten days later the captain was after an acting sub-lieutenant – with an emphasis on the acting – who was found sitting in the captain's sea shelter when he was second officer of the watch. The fact that the ship was enveloped in blinding rain and at anchor made not the slightest impression on the captain. Orders were orders, rules were rules, and disobedience was a punishable offence. He was determined to see that his men knew the full meaning of the word discipline.

It went on thus until May 1923 when Captain John Knowles Im Thurn CBE replaced Mackworth as captain of *Hood*.

Suddenly, as if by magic, the atmosphere of the ship was changed. It was not that *Hood* became any less a fighting ship; students of matter might have said she became a better ship because of the decline of unnecessary tension. She was certainly a happier ship after that day in May when Captain Mackworth was piped over the side for the last time.

That summer with *Repulse* and *Snapdragon*, *Hood* visited the Scandinavian countries again. In December with *Repulse* and five ships from the First Light Cruiser Squadron she set sail on a goodwill trip around the world.

They arrived in Capetown on 22 December in a dreadful summer squall. The acting governor-general arrived on board to a 19-gun salute, and the acting high commissioner came, to 17 guns.

They anchored in Table Bay and all hands were given leave. The ship was opened to visitors, this being one of the primary reasons for the voyage. It was part of the naval tradition, and very good politics, to have elements of the fleet in the far reaches of the empire from time to time.

Christmas, then, was a jolly time in South Africa, with the people vying to open their doors and entertain the officers and men. Captain Im Thurn was as generous as regulations allowed, the weather could have shown some improvement, but a tar must be ready for any of that, and the South African part of the voyage was a success in every way.

On 6 January they were in Durban, and on the twelfth they headed for Zanzibar where the Sultan honoured them with a visit.

Captain Im Thurn was, as noted, an easygoing man by comparison with his predecessor, but there were limits of discipline even so, and one day one of the ship's lesser officers felt the full fury of his wrath.

The bandmaster had got himself into difficult straits on shore leave and was feeling the pinch in the petty officer's mess. Someone gave him the idea of selling his motor bicycle by raffle. It seemed so capital a suggestion that he staged a raffle on the mess deck. He did well enough; the motor bicycle was duly awarded, the bandmaster pocketed the proceeds and all seemed well.

Then the captain heard about it. It was, of course, a total violation of King's regulations to pursue private business on one of His Majesty's vessels, and an even more serious violation to engage in public gambling. The bandmaster was definitely in trouble and might have been court-martialled for what he had done.

Fortunately for him Mackworth was no longer in charge of his destiny, for Captain Im Thurn meted out a punishment for this that Mackworth would have given for an unshined boot: he cautioned the bandmaster and sadly wrote him up in the log.

During the 1920s a succession of captains, lesser officers and ranks passed across the decks of *Hood*. Captain H. D. Reinold had her in 1925–6, followed by Captain W. F. French.

He was succeeded not by a captain, but by an officer in charge, Lieutenant-Commander W. M. Phipps-Hornby, who paid the ship off into dockyard control in 1929 when she went in for a refit and was out of service. She was out until 1931 when Captain J. F. C. Patterson took over the new commissioning and took her to sea once again, this time with the Atlantic Fleet.

The peacetime years were a happy time for the men of the Royal Navy. With *Repulse*, *Delhi*, *Norfolk* and *Dorsetshire*, *Hood* went to the West Indies in 1932, and then in the summer they went to Bangor and Guernsey and stopped in at a number of British ports to remind the people that the fleet was out there as the nation's first line of defence.

In the dockyard at Portsmouth, where she had been given her first major overhaul, the fitters and armourers had made many significant changes. *Hood* was moving with the times, and the times meant air power as never before. On this trip to the West Indies and back, *Hood* spent a good deal of time working up the new guns. Multiple pom-poms had been installed between the second and third batteries of the secondary guns, where before there had been boats.

By the time that *Hood* returned from her pleasant sojourn

of 1932 events were brewing in an unhappy world. In 1933 she went to Gibraltar again for wintering, and visited Tangiers. But it was not the same. There were rumours about and they were not pleasant ones.

Britain had reduced her naval might after the London Naval Conference of 1930. It was not long before the Germans began building a new fleet, a small one to begin with, but a start in a direction the world had once believed was restricted for ever.

Italy, too, was determined to have a navy to match Benito Mussolini's ambitions, and so as the British ships moved in the Mediterranean and elsewhere, more and more often they began to encounter those of other powers.

With the growth of military power came flexing of muscles. In 1934 *Hood* was with the Home Fleet and on exercises, when the strained relations on the German–Danish border caused cancellation of the Scandinavian tour. Something new, tension, had definitely been added to the Fleet programme that year.

Next year, the Anglo–German Naval Treaty permitted the Third Reich to begin building her navy in earnest. The treaty called for a German fleet that was 35 per cent as powerful as that of Britain, but one change after another – including outright cheating – made those requirements meaningless.

On the surface it was the same old routine. Captain F. J. B. Tower had *Hood* when they went to Arosa Bay in January before heading for Gibraltar and the usual round of exercises, fleet manœuvres and diplomatic appearances. The month was marred by the drowning of one of the ship's boys, James Maurice Brown, but that was the way of the Navy and of the sea; tragedy was never far off even in peacetime when men sailed out in ships.

In 1935 the Mediterranean was disrupted by the growlings and posturings of Benito Mussolini and the Fascists.

Hood and *Ramillies* were sent home from Gibraltar in a hurry after the Ethiopia crisis. Some of the crew got extended leave then, but it was not very long before 1936 brought *Hood* into the new world of European war, from which she would never again be very far removed.

The Spanish Civil War encouraged immense interest and deep involvement by the Germans and Italians on the one hand and the Russians on the other. Britain was committed to a difficult policy – non-intervention. What that meant not everybody aboard *Hood* or the other ships of the fleet quite knew, but it was the politicians who invented the idea; it meant difficulty without resolution.

On the way to Gibraltar, after another cruise to the West Indies, Captain Tower was suddenly called up when *Renown* collided with *Hood*. The cruiser had struck *Hood* on the starboard side aft and had caused a certain amount of damage.

There were no casualties, but there was a tremendous amount of agitation about it, as there always was when an accident harmed one of His Majesty's vessels. The damage was put to rights at Gibraltar and later at Portsmouth; the rest of it was sorted out by the Admiralty, in time for Captain Tower to take *Hood* back to sea that year.

She went to the Canaries and stopped at Las Palmas for water, provisions and some leave. Then she headed for Panama, and the Madeiras on her way home. It was a very successful trip.

In August she had another minor refit, home leave for the majority on board and a big change in officers and men. After this she headed for service with the Mediterranean fleet, Captain A. F. Pridham aboard, and flying an admiral's flag. She headed for Gibraltar again.

In autumn of 1936 *Hood* was still in the Mediterranean, this time at Malta. The following month she sailed from Valletta to Gibraltar on the fifth, and then on the eleventh moved on to Tangiers which was in troubled waters. There she encountered the German cruiser *Königsberg*, the Italian cruiser *Quento*, the French destroyer *Milan*, the German destroyer *Iltis* and the Italian destroyer *Aquila*. Then along came the German cruiser *Nürnberg*, to make quite an international fleet patrolling these unhappy waters.

Admiral Sir Geoffrey Blake, flying his flag in *Hood*, was directed to lead the Mediterranean fleet in protection of British shipping. That was all.

It seemed strange at Christmas time to be anchored in these waters, and then to come back to moor at Gibraltar and see the German *Graf Spee* come in. It was a strange world.

In the spring of 1937 the Spanish war took a new turn. The Germans and the Italians shipped war materials to Generalissimo Franco as they would, and then complained bitterly that the Loyalists were receiving supplies from the Soviets. That led to the *Thorpehill* incident, which involved a merchant ship declared free of war materials, which was stopped on the high seas by Spanish Insurgent (Fascist) vessels.

ss *Thorpehill* was on her way to Bilbao, when the Insurgent cruiser *Almirante Cervera* and the armed trawler *Galerna* overhauled her and demanded that she stop and be searched. The captain of the *Thorpehill* immediately had his radio operator busy calling up the fleet. The word was received by *Hood* and by the county-class cruiser *Shropshire* which met north of Bilbao, with the announced intention of making sure that His Majesty's merchant shipping was left alone.

The incident might have been nasty, except that when three British destroyers appeared on the scene, the Spaniards withdrew rather than force an international incident. The blockade of Bilbao continued, however, for the Fascists were determined to stop the inflow of supplies to the Loyalists no matter how they did it.

The British destroyers involved in the *Thorpehill* incident were based at St Jean-de-Luz, and to this port *Hood* now came to drop anchor and show her magnificent presence. For it was from this point that the ships took off to brave the Insurgent air and sea gauntlet to carry supplies to Bilbao.

One day the British merchant ships *Mansterley*, *Stanbrook* and *MacGregor* decided that they would run the gauntlet and *Hood* was to go along and provide a screen for them. It was a brave measure for the day; the Chamberlain government was anxious to do almost anything to avoid a confrontation that might lead to general war (and given Britain's state of defence perhaps they were right). But the Chamberlain government had wavered to the extent that the integrity of the Royal Navy had been brought into question, and strong representations had been made that forced the government to action. The action would be a show of force to indicate that Britain would indeed protect the ships that flew her flag.

Thus when the three merchant vessels set out on the night of 21 April, *Hood* headed out for sea too. It was no coincidence.

As morning came on the misty Vizcayan coast, the three merchant ships moved in line toward Bilbao. The challenge might not come in such heavy fog, at least the merchant captains could hope for that, for they were the exposed ones.

When they reached the mouth of the Nervion and were ten miles off Punta de la Galea, they were warned by the British destroyer *Firedrake* that Franco's warships were waiting for them. The food the ships carried for Bilbao was contraband.

As long as the ships were outside the three-mile limit they were safe: that was international practice and had been for many years. But the Franco ships, *Almirante Cervera* and *Galerna*, were waiting outside, determined that the food would not pass.

Vice-Admiral Blake had his instructions, and for once they were to a seaman's liking. The ships would not be interfered with in international waters. *Hood* was there, on hand, to see that this was so, and *Hood* was known throughout the world as the greatest and finest sea-fighting instrument afloat.

The first move was made by *Almirante Cervera*. Her commander called up *MacGregor*, the leading merchant ship, and ordered the captain to heave to. Instead, the captain sent an SOS, and *Firedrake* summoned *Hood*, which came moving up majestically. Vice-Admiral Blake addressed the commander of the Spanish Insurgent cruiser. The Franco forces would please not interfere with British shipping outside territorial waters.

'Our territorial waters extend six miles off the coast,' said the commander of *Almirante Cervera*.

Hood was at quarters. Her 15-inch guns were silent, but ready. The men of the ship had been instructed to be ready as well, and they were.

'I do not recognize your claim,' said Admiral Blake. Then he turned to the merchant ship *MacGregor* and said, 'Proceed if you wish.'

MacGregor and the other two merchant ships did proceed past the watchful but silent guns of the hostile Spanish ships and into Bilbao harbour, where another of the Spanish claims was proved to be a lie: the harbour was not mined as the Insurgents had claimed.

The incident of Bilbao became history and not a shot was fired. If it did not affect the outcome of the war, that was a matter of British policy that transcended the ability of the Royal Navy to manage affairs. It was, after all, the politicians and not the Navy who decided policy.

That was the way it had to be, and in these years of the late 1930s much as navy men might complain in private about the inactivity of the government, they kept a taut ship aboard *Hood*, and did their duty manfully. British honour, British pride and British mercantilism were all threatened by the Spanish. *Hood* and *Shropshire* continued to make a show of force, and they made their rendezvous fifty miles north of Bilbao under orders to protect British interests.

The furore died down quickly enough and within two weeks the *Hood* was called back to Portsmouth. But there had been a taste of the future here, an indication that the Spanish War was going to heat the Mediterranean and might spill over into the Atlantic and the North Sea.

Hood's spring was quiet enough that year. She went to Spithead on 11 May and was decked out there for the coronation of King George VI and Queen Elizabeth. The highlight of that event came on 20 May, when His Majesty visited the fleet.

All this while of course, serious business was at hand in London. Anthony Eden was doing his utmost to guarantee non-intervention in Spain, while the Germans, the Italians and the Russians were knee-deep in the war. So too were the emotions of many liberals some of whom joined the fight. Fine lives were lost in the international brigades and in other units. Young men who went to fight often set out for ideals that probably did not really exist.

The British government was well aware of all the difficulties, but felt impelled to confine its own role to the protection of British commerce.

The role became ever more difficult as the Franco forces – and the Germans and Italians – bombed neutral ships whenever they had the slightest suspicion that they might be carrying supplies for the Loyalists.

Vice-Admiral Blake had a new command, he was to be senior officer commanding the Western Basin. That meant there would be responsibilities involving Marseilles, Barcelona and the Balearic islands.

At the beginning of January 1938 Vice-Admiral A. B.

Cunningham took over the Battle-Cruiser Squadron with his flag in *Hood*. She left Malta on Wednesday, 5 January, and headed out to sea for practice with the 15-inch guns. Two days later she arrived in Palma de Majorca and the admiral took over his new command.

Hood remained in Palma only a few days. She waited until *Devonshire* arrived from the port of Marseille with mail for the fleet and with Sir Norman King KCMG aboard. Sir Norman was HBM Consul-General, destined for Barcelona, and in order to make a suitable impression *Hood* would take him there.

She sailed on 11 January. At Barcelona, the admiral learned that the Dutch steamer *Hannah* had been sunk that day six miles southeast of Cape San Antonio. This was a matter of considerable concern to Cunningham, particularly since there was deep suspicion that she had been sunk by a German or an Italian submarine. There was nothing to be done about it, however.

Hood remained in Barcelona for two days, and then headed for Valencia before returning to Palma.

The admiral had many duties. Not the least of them was the entertainment of officers from various other navies, with a fine eye to their behaviour and what it might reflect in the attitude of their government. That week he dined in the admiral's cabin aboard *Hood* with Ammiraglio di Divisione Conte Alberto Marenco di Moriondo, the senior representative of Mussolini's Navy, who brought his flag-captain and his staff to the affair.

The Italians seemed friendly, which had not been the case the last time Cunningham had encountered them. The Admiral suggested the oddities of the sinking of the Dutch steamer, and wondered if the submarine could by any chance have been one of Moriondo's.

The Italian admiral said he would investigate. In fact nothing really came of it, as indeed everyone expected.

However, the Italians were warned that the sinking had come far too close to the British patrol zone for their liking.

Hood next went to Marseille, but the admiral kept track of everything in the area by radio. Franco's planes were bombing Valencia regularly, and the British consulate was nearly hit on 20 January. Three days later the Insurgent fleet was bombarding Valencia from the sea, and a number of shells again fell close to the consulate. The consul protested, the Franco navy men said they would be more careful in the future, and Admiral Cunningham took note of it all.

What disturbed him more that week was another submarine incident. The British freighter ss *Clonlara* reported she was attacked by an unidentified submarine ten miles north of Castellon de la Plana. She escaped damage, but not so ss *Thorpness*, which was bombed at Tarragona with two British sailors killed, seven wounded and five missing.

A week later came another submarine report: the ss *Lake Geneva*, a British ship, was attacked by an unknown submarine just over three miles southeast of Valencia. One torpedo passed under the ship, the submarine began to surface, the conning tower came up, and then her captain changed his mind – perhaps he saw the Union Jack – submerged and disappeared.

These attacks called for action. Admiral Cunningham returned to Palma, where he sought an interview with Vice-Admiral Francisco Moreno, commander of Franco's forces. He warned the Spanish admiral of Britain's concern and in return received assurances. But he could get no information on the identity of the submarine that had fired on the British vessels. All Moreno would say was that he had just issued orders to his forces not to attack British ships.

The war for the Loyalists was going badly, and Admiral Cunningham reported on it to the Admiralty in his regular letters. The air raids were growing more frequent, the casualties heavier.

What he must concern himself with, of course, were British interests. It was all very well to be sympathetic to the people of the war-torn cities, but British interests were paramount. How little the Spanish Insurgent promises meant was understood on 31 January when the admiral learned that the British steamer ss *Endymion* had been sunk sixteen miles south of Cape Tinoso.

Grimly, Admiral Cunningham moved into action. He ordered a sweep by three destroyers just outside the three-mile limit in that area, making a demonstration of strength and looking for the offending submarine.

Then, when the sweep was over, he directed that regular patrols be established ten miles off the coast. He also demanded further explanations from Admiral Moreno. The admiral told a strange story. The ships that had been attacked but not sunk had been attacked by Spanish submarines in violation of orders. But those that were sunk were not attacked by the Insurgents. However, Admiral Cunningham, who knew better from agents ashore, listened and said nothing. That was all his orders permitted him to do.

Hood soon left Spanish waters for Malta and other duties, but she was back again with the admiral at the end of March. Palma was now the major base of operations of the Spanish Insurgent fleet, and sixteen of Franco's naval vessels were in the harbour, plus two Italian destroyers and Ammiraglio Moriondo's flagship the cruiser *Quarto*.

The admiral had to stand by and watch the operations of the Italians and the Spanish Insurgents. Shortly after he arrived, the Spanish transport *Marques de Comillas* arrived along with the ss *Ebro*, escorted by two gunboats. They came in, heavily laden, and landed war materials that obviously came from Italy.

The ease with which Franco's forces controlled the seas gave a foretaste of the end of the war, even more than the bombings of Barcelona and Valencia.

By the first of April it was apparent that the situation of the Loyalist government in Barcelona was worsening rapidly. The admiral in *Hood* left Palma and moved to Caldetas to confer with the British minister. He took stores for the embassy and consulate in *Hood* to Barcelona. He then sailed for Valencia, having picked up Seaman Neil Inskter, formerly of the ss *Sarastone*, a distressed British seaman who had been in a Barcelona hospital that was under bombardment.

The evacuation of refugees was now in full swing, and *Hood* at Valencia helped. The admiral made arrangements for the evacuation of refugees from El Perello, about eleven miles southwest of Valencia. There were still many British nationals in residence in war-torn Spain and they had to be looked after.

In conference with the consul and other authorities, the admiral gained the impression that the situation was easing. After the strong display off the coast by the destroyers, he could at least hope that no more British vessels would be attacked.

At the end of the month *Hood* was off again, headed for Gibraltar and then Malta, and she kept going back and forth all that summer. In August, Vice-Admiral Cunningham was succeeded by Vice-Admiral Layton as commander of the force. *Hood* continued in her duties, the symbol of Britain's naval power, to be shown to those along the Spanish coast who might be forgetful of British interests.

Next year, the men who watched over the ships at Whitehall proposed to give *Hood* a good face-lift. She was going to have a complete overhaul of her secondary armament. Modern 5·25-inch dual purpose mountings would be installed and these would let her use the guns for both anti-

aircraft and naval firing. She would also get rid of the tor-
pedo-tubes that were no longer in fashion, and she would
get an aircraft hangar, more armour and new propulsion
machinery.

Added up, it would have brought her very much up-to-
date by the standards of the fleet and made a stronger
fighting machine of her for modern warfare. But when 1939
came the international situation was such that the idea of
laying up *Hood* was unthinkable. All that could be done was
to give her new 4-inch anti-aircraft guns, and more small
ones, around the conning-tower and the after control station.

Had the original changes been possible, it is doubtful if
they would have affected her metacentric balance. But the
way the quick changes were made, the effect was to increase
her top weight and make her very heavy. The result was that
in a sea of any kind waves swept across the quarter-deck and
even along the boat-deck. Her weight had increased from
45,000 tons to 48,000 tons.

In the spring of 1939, however, as anyone in the Admiralty
knew, there was no time to do anything about that.

5

The Waves of War

January began the process of doing what could be done to make *Hood* right for the tasks that might be assigned to her. The refitting began then, and also such rearming as was possible to give her in those worrying circumstances. Hitler and his new navy posed a real threat to the Royal Navy.

During the years following the occupation of the Rhineland Hitler had been building a new German fleet. Rather, his admirals had been doing it, for Hitler really had little confidence in a navy for his or Germany's purposes.

He was never more than half convinced that the fleet he would have could turn the tide of war. But Admiral Raeder was persuasive as were others. In the general rearmament it was certain that the Germans would have to do something to counter the power of the British Fleet. Submarines alone were not considered adequate.

Thus the German navy boasted *Scharnhorst* and *Gneisenau*, a pair of modern battle-cruisers with nine 11-inch modern guns, as compared, for example, to *Hood*'s eight 15-inch guns. More important than these heavy ships were the two battleships that were almost finished, *Tirpitz* and *Bismarck*.

Bismarck, oddly enough, was in the ways as *Hood* was undergoing her refurbishment. She was launched by Blohm and Voss of Hamburg on St Valentine's Day 1939, and such was the glory preceding her that she was given the kind of send-off reserved for heroes. Admiral Raeder, Goering, Goebbels, a clutch of generals, political advisers and all the Nazi notables, were on the podium as Hitler unleashed his oratory and declared that this marvellous vessel would recreate the spirit of the great Chancellor. The bands played stirring naval tunes and the Nazi flags flew in all their ominous portent. Dorothea von Loewenfeld, the granddaughter of the Chancellor, christened the grand ship in his name.

Bismarck was a sixth of a mile long and more than 100 feet wide. When fully laden she would be 50,000 tons, compared with *Hood*'s soggy 48,000 tons, she had eight 15-inch guns of the most modern design and could carry six aircraft. She had 13-inch armour on her turrets and sides, and she was without doubt the most powerful warship afloat.

England, of course, did not know this fact, at least the England outside the intelligence community which knew some of it and guessed at more. Officially *Bismarck* was listed as 35,000 tons in order to comply with the announced standards of the London Naval Treaty. In fact most of England knew nothing, or next to nothing, about *Bismarck* or the German Navy.

Admiral Raeder had a fine plan for a fleet. Called the Z plan, he had been working on it for several years. He had not done badly, considering the Nazis and their highly political approach to everything. He had the battle-cruisers, he had two battleships building, three pocket battleships, three heavy cruisers, a half-dozen light cruisers, destroyers and some sixty u-boats.

The Z plan called for him to have a fleet by 1944 that could safely challenge the British fleet as it then was. For the new German Navy would also have four aircraft-carriers, eight battleships like *Bismarck* and everything else scaled in the same grand manner.

Spring came and *Bismarck* was being fitted out. Across the Channel *Hood* was returning to the fleet, still acclaimed as the greatest fighting ship afloat. She had been that for so long that no one thought of disputing the claim.

The Admiralty, building *Prince of Wales*, knew that *Hood*'s birthday indicated her deficiencies in modern times, but the spring of 1939 was no time to talk about that. *Hood* got as much as Whitehall could give her in the short time available, and she went back to join the fleet.

August was a tense month and *Hood* was having as much of a dockyard refit as could be managed. It was the eleventh of the month before she was out at sea on manœuvres, training a green crew and in a sense working up all over again. It was darken ship and light up ship and all the other drills; exercises with the carrier *Courageous*, and HMS *Sturdy*, practising action stations, zigzag patterns and all the rest.

There were little tragedies. Ordinary Signalman Donald Charles Proctor died of peritonitis on 21 August. But there were 1,400 live and lively men aboard, and some 90 officers to train them and make them ready for the ordeal that seemed now almost certain to be ahead.

On 1 September *Hood* was at sea and at action stations at 0400 hours, and then many times throughout the nervous day. On the third came the news of the declaration of war against Germany. The Captain announced it over the speaker system. So now when they zigzagged, or when they sent a destroyer to stop and look over a fishing-boat, there was a reason. All things that had been practice before now became work in deadly earnest, as every man knew.

Hood was in constant danger when at sea. On 5 September she had her first encounter with the enemy. At 1225 hours a look-out shouted, 'Torpedo track!'

Hood was swung hard a-port, the torpedoes missed, and the destroyers with her began to search for the contact. They searched, they chased, and *Hood* resumed her course.

Often enough there were contacts now, and plenty of work to do. She sent *Fury* out to check on one contact

picked up by Asdic on the eighth, and then two days later
was investigating a Swedish oiler. Was she Swedish, or was
she a German masquerading as such? *Fearless* checked that
one out, and another merchant ship the same day, and
reported back to *Hood*.

There were signs of the tragedy all around them. On the
eleventh they were out and *Fearless* was detached to search
for the boats of ss *Kirby*, which had been sunk by u-boats
off the Faeroes.

On 12 September they were back at Scapa Flow, and
recreation parties went ashore that day and the next. The
oil-tanker *Wardware* came alongside and *Hood* was oiled.
The men on watch washed down the ship. They took on
about 100 bags of potatoes and 1,702 lbs of cabbage. She
was a big ship with a big appetite. Back to sea on 14 September,
to Loch Ewe this time, and then back to Scapa Flow for
3,000 lbs of meat and eight bags of mail.

A rest-up in Scapa for a week, and then back to sea on
22 September, when *Fortune* made a submarine contact at
1320 hours and *Firedrake* confirmed it. It was zigzag, and
22 knots in fast turns for an hour, and then action stations.
On the twenty-third *Express* sighted a mine off to port of
Hood and came up gingerly and exploded it. They were back
in Scapa Flow on Sunday, 24 September. The admiral
inspected the lower deck and made a speech to the men about
the war and their duty. Everyone knew about the war and
most men knew their duty. It meant such things as: leave
for the port watch, but not for the anti-aircraft gunners. It
was war all right.

The work was anything but glamorous. It involved long
days and nights in the merciless pounding seas, sealing off
the approaches to the North Sea so that the German merchant
vessels could not sneak home, and so that German
raiders could not sneak out to prey on British commerce as
they had done so dreadfully in the last war.

Hood was a grim grey now, her once white decks and woodwork dull as the sky about them, all the pianos and hangings and little niceties of shipboard life in peacetime stripped away to conform with King's regulations.

She flew the flag of Vice-Admiral W. J. Whitworth, and she undertook the hazardous, routine duty of protecting and guarding the sea lanes. There was a point in it all: the Germans must not be allowed to escape and roam the seas.

Day in and day out the major elements of the fleet were in those northern waters, cruising, watching and guarding. Sometimes it was the North Sea. Sometimes it was the North Atlantic.

There came a bit of excitement on 25 September when the submarine *Spearfish* was reported to be badly damaged, lying off Horn Reefs near the Dogger Bank and unable to dive. Her position was close to the spot where Admiral Beatty had encountered Admiral Hipper and fought the action that kept the Kaiser's *Hochseeflotte* bottled up for the remainder of the last war.

Admiral Forbes, Commander-in-Chief of the Home Fleet, sent the Second Cruiser Squadron, a number of destroyers, the Eighteenth Cruiser Squadron and *Hood* and *Repulse* out to provide cover for her rescue. The admiral was not taking any chances on being accused of forgetting the lessons of history.

But history was not repeating itself precisely. This was a different war and it took on different aspects.

Spearfish was rescued from her uncomfortable position and the admiral sent destroyers to take her home. But in the course of this operation, the capital ships were sighted by German observation planes, the big Heinkel flying boats that were to poke about and pry around the ports of England for the next few years. Marshal Goering's Luftwaffe was notified, a coastal bombing squadron was alerted, and a handful of two-engined Heinkel bombers came to attack the big ships and sink them if they could.

The Heinkels came in. The pom-poms began to send their smoke-puffs up into the air from the decks of *Hood*, and the new big anti-aircraft guns joined in.

The Heinkels loosed their bombs and very nearly hit *Ark Royal*, but not quite. They did have more luck with *Hood*, both good and bad. One German bomber demonstrated his skills well enough when a bomb came searing down and struck *Hood* on the quarter. It was only a glancing blow and perhaps for that reason the bomb did not explode, but fell harmlessly into the sea. No one was hurt, except the feelings of the anti-aircraft gunners and their gunnery officers, who were rated for the ineffectuality of the fire they put up. It was not only that, the volume of fire was not strong enough to do the job. Then it was back to base.

There followed a succession of missions of the sort to which most of the major ships were assigned: to keep the sea lanes open for British shipping, suppress the submarine menace where possible, and prevent Germany's capital ships from moving in the North Sea and the Atlantic.

Of course they were not always successful. The *Graf Spee* and other raiders got out into the Atlantic, and wreaked havoc until they were either forced back home by oil starvation or were trapped, as was the *Graf Spee*, and dealt with in shores far from Europe.

The existence of *Hood, Repulse, Renown* and all the rest in these waters was the grand deterrent to Hitler's navy, and everybody knew that. So if the war for the 1,500 officers and men jammed aboard the great, grey ship had seemed dull previously, they were now serving the most useful of purposes.

Sometimes there was plenty of excitement, as in October when they went after the battle-cruiser *Gneisenau*. This German warship was spotted steaming north out of the

Skagerrak on 8 October by aircraft of Coastal Command. The report said that the big ship was accompanied by the heavy cruiser *Köln* and a destroyer escort. It seemed that an effort was being made to break through the blockade, round the coast of Scotland to the north, and escape out into the Atlantic.

In fact, the German high command was doing something quite different. Admiral Raeder had authorized an attempt to draw some of the Home Fleet into waters far enough off-shore that Goering's bombers could deal with them. Goering boasted that his Luftwaffe could handle the Royal Navy if it were given a little co-operation. Goering's boasts had not yet been tested in the fires and found to be leaden.

So *Hood* and *Repulse* were sent out to the northern approaches to Bergen to stop any flanking movements by the Germans. By the time they were speeding through the sea towards their target, the target had already turned about and was heading back into the safety of the Kattegat. The German operation had not succeeded and because of that *Hood*'s interception came to nothing. With such high hopes they had set out, the rumours flying about the decks and messes. They were going to get themselves a German this time.

By 10 October no news of the enemy had been received so that the admiral altered course for the Butt of Lewis. Just before 1500 hours the admiral received word: early that morning the Germans had passed through the Great Belt and were heading south. The chase was over.

Royal Oak was sent back to Scapa Flow, other vessels sent to various bases, while the admiral headed for Loch Ewe with *Rodney*, *Hood* and six destroyers.

Thus neither he nor *Hood* were on hand at Scapa Flow on 14 October, when German submarine commander Günther Prien penetrated the inner precincts of the naval base and torpedoed *Royal Oak* at anchor off the northeast shore. The

loss of life was dreadful, including Rear-Admiral Henry
E. C. Blagvore.

The whole Home Fleet operation was disturbed by this
event. For if the Germans could penetrate the base at will
then it was no longer a base. Immediately *Aurora*, *Belfast*,
Curlew and most of the fleet auxiliaries were ordered to
Loch Ewe, that lonely place, which would be their base
until the entrances to Scapa Flow could be made safe.

Hood had no time to worry, however, for there was too
much doing. On the evening of 15 October, along with
Nelson, *Rodney*, *Furious*, *Aurora*, *Belfast* and nine destroyers, she
was despatched to find the Northern Patrol and assist in the
interception of a number of German merchant ships that
seemed to be making their way back to Germany by way of
the Denmark Strait. Off they went to hunt.

The destroyers were fuelled at sea by the big ships to keep
the hunt going longer. That was in the Arctic Circle on 17
October. But no enemy merchantmen were found and the
searchers turned homewards. Then one ship was captured,
and one was scuttled by her crew to avoid capture by the
armed merchant cruisers of the patrol. So the voyage had
not been a waste of time.

Hood was lucky in her timing these days. She had just
missed the *Royal Oak* tragedy, and while she was out on the
merchant ship hunt, the Germans carried on air raids in
strength against Rosyth and Scapa Flow, the targets being
the ships. At Rosyth *Southampton* was hit by one bomb and
suffered a number of casualties. At Scapa Flow the *Iron Duke*
was damaged by a near miss and had to be beached.

The enemy did not get away unscathed, three bombers
were shot down at Rosyth and one at Scapa Flow. But even
that was not enough: the Admiralty now knew that the air
raid defences of the fleet were much too weak.

Hood anchored in Loch Ewe. Some days she went out for
short runs, some days she went on longer ones; sometimes

she had assignments that took her out for days; and she moved back and forth from Plymouth to Rosyth and points around the north.

Late in October she set out with *Rodney* and *Nelson* as part of a covering force for a convoy carrying iron ore from Narvik to the Firth of Forth. That was hazardous but essential duty as Norwegian iron was precious for the foundries of Britain.

The big ships went out to poke about in the recesses along the Norwegian coast. They made for the Lofoten Islands. In the stormy weather the navigator and the engineers became concerned about the way in which *Hood* responded to heavy seas. The swells boomed over her quarter-deck, tons upon tons of briny water pushing her stern down, and it was only with real difficulty that she came up again. The pressure worked on her frames, plating and superstructure all at once. As they said in the engine room, the old girl's age was beginning to show.

The heavy ships stayed out until 31 October and then they pulled in at Greenock. There the admiral received word of the activity he and *Hood* had missed. Once the convoy had reached Kinnaird Head, HMS *Somali* had discovered a German submarine, attacked, and with the help of HMS *Tartar* managed to sink it. *Hood* had missed all the excitement.

The need for her and her kind, however, was shown irrevocably when *Graf Spee* left the Indian Ocean for the Atlantic, and the German Admiralty sent out *Scharnhorst* and *Gneisenau* to divert attention from this manœuvre.

They were led out at the end of the third week of November by Admiral Marschall in *Scharnhorst* and headed north for the Skagerrak and beyond. They were discovered by the auxiliary cruiser *Rawalpindi*, an armed merchant vessel, which came upon the ships unawares on the morning of 22 November about halfway between the Faeroes and Iceland.

Rawalpindi carried seven 6-inch guns, which was quite

enough for patrol duties and possible fights with armed merchant ships or even submarines. But 6-inch guns were as nothing to the eighteen 11-inch guns pitted against her now. Obviously she was outmatched, and yet Captain E. C. Kennedy fought. He was hampered both by the guns and by the speed differential. His ship made only 17 knots while the Germans made more than 30 knots. The outcome was never in doubt. *Rawalpindi* was hit, holed, set on fire and finally sunk. Most of her crew were lost.

However, her warning had set the wheels in motion in Whitehall and across the north. The Home Fleet sailed to cover the routes the German ships might be expected to follow as a passage into the Atlantic.

Once again they had no such intention. Admiral Marschall had his orders. Having accomplished the ruse, he headed back for the Skagerrak and soon enough was safe within the confines of the River Jade and Germany's great naval base.

Now came an event that was to be of ironic consequence in the life of *Hood*. When the orders came and the fleet went out to cut off the German battleships, *Hood* was at Plymouth with Vice-Admiral Whitworth aboard. Meanwhile, from the French shore the French battle-cruiser *Dunkerque* and the cruisers *Georges-Leygues* and *Montcalm* had sailed. There was to be a combined operation for the navies of the two Channel allies.

Since Vice-Admiral Gensoul, the French commander, was senior officer present, he took over. The forces made rendezvous in mid-Channel, and headed up towards Iceland, sailing west and north.

Dunkerque, a smaller vessel than *Hood* armed with 13-inch guns, took the lead. *Hood*, the behemoth, kept station on the smaller French ship and the rest of the force came along behind.

Nothing happened, for the birds had never really tried to

fly the coop after all, and so early in December the combined operation was over, and *Hood* headed for Loch Ewe to refuel and await new orders.

The fleet had its problems that winter, following the penetration of Scapa Flow by German U-boats and the torpedoing of *Royal Oak*. *Hood* had her own special problems, and they were serious ones.

The worst of them was the burden of change, and what the quick wartime changes had done to her speed and manœuvreability. She was down to 25 knots now and she behaved very badly in heavy seas. But there was the fate of *Royal Oak*, and *Nelson* had been badly damaged by a German mine while entering Loch Ewe the day after *Hood* had come back from her fruitless chase of *Scharnhorst* and *Gneisenau*. Then *Rodney* was found to be in a more advanced state of decrepitude than *Hood*, and she had first priority for refitting. Admiral Forbes had no recourse but to keep *Hood* in service. She was the biggest and most powerful ship and the only major unit he had to work with this difficult winter.

She went to sea that December to give cover to the first incoming convoy of Canadian troops. That milestone convoy had set out from Halifax to bring these troops from the Empire to Britain's aid in the time of crisis. The Admiralty was anxious that all go well, that the Germans not get wind of the convoy at all and that if they did they not be permitted to interfere with it. On 10 December *Furious*, *Repulse*, *Emerald*, *Hunter* and *Hyperion* were sent out from Halifax to sweep ahead and eliminate any menace.

It was so cold that *Furious* could not operate her aircraft because of the failure of the hydraulic system. It took a full day to thaw it out and repair it, and the planes did not begin flying until 11 December.

Then they ran into heavy weather. Fog grounded the aircraft, or rather decked them on the carrier. It fell, fortunately, just after the last flight of the day had returned.

It was like this all the way across the 'pond'; the ships were lucky when visibility was three miles. But there were no incidents until the very end, when at about 0430 hours of 17 December *Furious* and *Aquitania* collided with the ss *Samaria*, a darkened ship steaming on an opposite course. *Hood* stood by and then came back to port.

She was at sea again on Christmas Day, searching for the enemy and protecting Britain's shore. She was out again on New Year's Day, braving the cold, the winds and the hard storms of winter.

They worked her like a scow these days, for they had so little else. She hardly seemed to drop anchor in Greenock or Loch Ewe, before she was ordered out once again to strengthen the thin line of ships that guarded the Atlantic approaches.

As winter dragged on the contribution to the war effort of the Norwegian iron ores, and of Norway generally, was threatened by the German invasion. The British government decided on a counterstroke.

On 2 March *Hood*, *Valiant* and six destroyers sailed to the north to provide assistance to forces on Norwegian convoy duty and patrol. Five days later *Hood* and *Valiant* were at Scapa Flow. Winston Churchill, the First Lord of the Admiralty, was aboard *Rodney*, which was prevented from entering the harbour by a mine threat. The First Lord was taken aboard *Hood*, therefore, while *Rodney* stayed at sea and the passage was swept.

These were hard times at Scapa Flow, for the Germans were concentrating air attacks here, trying to knock out some of the capital ships. Consequently the big ships were sent to sea time and time again, so that they would not be caught in the harbour without room to manœuvre. *Hood* was lucky. She kept missing the attacks, as on 16 March when a formation of three planes came over to bomb.

Rodney, *Renown* and *Norfolk* came under attack. The

aircraft each dropped 511-lb bombs. *Norfolk* was hit on the quarter-deck near Y turret. The bomb passed down through the upper, main and lower decks, exploded near Y shell room and blew a hole in the starboard side of the ship. Worse still, the hole was underwater, and then a fire started. So x and y magazines had to be flooded for safety. In that same attack *Iron Duke* was a target once again and suffered three near misses.

That day went down in British history in its own way. Following on this two attacks were made on shore targets, one at Hatston and one at Bridge of Wraith. At Bridge of Wraith one civilian was killed, four were wounded and some cottages were damaged. It accomplished little for the Germans, except for one thing: it was the first attack on the civilian population and had caused the first civilian casualties of the war in the United Kingdom. It was a taste of the horror to come.

6

Hood's *Men in Norway*

From the beginning of the war, Hitler had tried to keep the Scandinavian states within his orbit. However, early in 1940 it became apparent that they were slipping. Britain was receiving supplies of ores and other valuables from Norway and Sweden. Denmark was not as firmly under control as the German High Command wanted. So the decision was made in Berlin to seize command of Scandinavia.

It became apparent that something was 'rotten' in Denmark and elsewhere when on 8 April a German transport crammed with troops was sunk by a British submarine off Lillesand and a German flotilla was reported steaming through the Great Belt. Then at dawn on 9 April, over a thousand-mile stretch of land, the Germans closed in on Norway and Denmark.

All this, and the sudden increase of air raids at Scapa Flow in recent weeks, began to come together. The fleet by this time was already on the move, for the Admiralty had received word from British reconnaissance planes that German battle-cruisers were moving north off Heligoland.

Through bad fortune the Home Fleet missed the Germans. Only the destroyer *Glowworm* found them, and she was quickly sunk before she could report that she had run into *Hipper* and *Scharnhorst*.

On 9 April, *Renown* found *Scharnhorst* in a blinding snowstorm, but lost her again when the Germans escaped behind a smoke screen. Next day Captain Warburton-Lee and his flotilla of five destroyers attacked the Germans at Narvik. It was a celebrated but disastrous action, which did much to destroy the enemy's potential there. Then on 13 April nine British destroyers sank three Germans and caused four others to flee and beach themselves as the crews deserted them. That German force was knocked out and so was Germany's hope of supplying Narvik from the sea.

Meanwhile in London Winston Churchill had committed Britain to Norway's assistance. But what could he use for troops? The fact was that Britain's manpower reserves were virtually exhausted, but fighting men had to be rushed to Norway if she were to be saved.

The Germans had not established communications between their main body and the garrisons on the coast of Norway by the end of the first week in April. The Norwegians were to hold them another week.

The British decided they would try to take Trondheim from the rear. This port was the key to the whole operation, for from Trondheim access would be available to all Norway's southern communications system. An army could secure a foothold here, establish a line which would cut off the south from the north, and offer a base where the Allied forces could sweep down the central plateau to control the coast.

Looking about for men to throw into the breach immediately, and particularly at Namsos and Andalsnes, the leaders of the war effort seized upon the men of the ships, the great ships, which could operate at least for a time with reduced crews. This reservoir, if one could call it that, provided strong, stout fighting men who must be used. There was no time to wait if the positions were to be taken and the Germans cut off.

Hood was called upon to contribute her force. Some 250 of her marines and other ranks were assembled. The loss was not serious to *Hood* in this case, for she was refitting at Plymouth. Lieutenant-Commander C. A. Awdry led this group into action. It was to be called Operation Primrose. They were to seize Andalsnes.

Lieutenant-Commander Awdry was called up to London post-haste, with orders to proceed to Andalsnes by ship. At midnight on 13 April they boarded a special train at Devonport which carried them to Rosyth, arriving at 1900 hours the following evening. They boarded the HMS *Black Swan* there with equipment and stores to carry them through a month. At the end of that time Whitehall expected them to have established a supply system.

The naval contingent was carried in four ships, *Black Swan*, *Bittern*, *Flamingo* and *Auckland*. They sailed in very bad weather on the morning of 15 April, but were soon forced to put into Invergordon and spend the night there. It was too nasty to go on.

This was, in a way, a godsend, for it enabled the officers of the various units to get together for the first time and make some plans for the operations ahead.

At 1000 hours on 16 April they sailed out of Invergordon. The orders were to proceed to Andalsnes, seize and occupy the town, which was the rail head for the line running to Dombas north to Trondheim and south to Lillehammer. Another contingent was to be landed at Alesund with 4-inch guns.

So they set out. From the beginning it was a shoe-string operation. They had no maps and all the information they had been given about Andalsnes came out of the instructions for pilotage in Norwegian waters.

For Alesund at least they had three photographs and two general maps. They knew virtually nothing about the terrain they were entering, the weather and the nature of the inhabitants, all the facts that an army's intelligence organization puts together before any sort of an attack. They were moving blind. It was an indication of the panic into which they had stepped.

They had one advantage and that alone. To the staff came Lieutenant M. Linge of the 11th Norwegian Regiment. And he knew something about the area.

They arrived at Andalsnes on the night of 17 April, and the *Hood* men in *Black Swan* came up alongside the jetty. The marines and the seamen came ashore and then began disembarking their stores. *Nelson*'s men followed them.

It was as easy as eating jam. The Germans were not about and seemed never to have been heard of. The Norwegians greeted the British contingent as if they were long lost brothers and vied among themselves for the privilege of bedding men down for the night. The *Hood*'s marines then were sent off to operate as one unit, and the seamen as another.

Next day the officers conferred with the Norwegians and decided there were too many men in the town. German observation planes flying over were bound to notice so much activity as was likely to occur. *Hood*'s sailors, therefore, were sent off five miles to another little place, while *Nelson*'s men stayed on in the town to provide working parties to unload ships that might come in and undertake other chores.

Hood's seamen had a hard time of it at first, for the Norwegian nights were freezing cold, and the camp to which they had been sent was used by the Norwegians only in summer. But the wooden huts were soon made tight, wood was brought in for fires and they bedded down quite nicely.

The camp was a busy place. The Norwegians came and went – the irregulars – and then occasionally some elements of the Norwegian army showed up. So there was always something new happening.

Hood's seamen worked in conjunction with a contingent

of marines from *Nelson*, and they yarned with them and drank beer with them when they could find it. But it was not a beer and skittles party at all, it was deadly earnest warfare. The officer in charge lined up the seamen and gave them close order infantry drill and then lectures on the care and use of the rifle. It was a short musketry course, and it taught them things some had never known and others had long forgotten. Lieutenant-Commander Awdry was a good officer.

On 17 April Awdry despatched Sub-Lieutenant D. C. Salter with the ship's howitzer for more warlike duty. At 0800 hours one petty officer and eighteen seamen from *Hood* assembled on the jetty at Andalsnes. The howitzer was loaded on to a rail wagon with 120 rounds of 3·7-inch ammunition.

Colonel Simpson, commander of the Royal Marines in the area, gave Salter his orders: he was to travel by train to Dombas and to report to the Norwegian headquarters there. Captain Allan of the Navy mission accompanied them on the journey. They set off through the frosty air, the wagon and one coach attached to a locomotive. The coach rattled on the tracks and steam came up from the locomotive as they moved along.

They arrived at the station at about noon, but they remained in the shelter of the rail-yard for several hours because German planes were flying overhead continuously. It was 1900 hours before they could disembark and move out of the station.

Salter went to Norwegian Army headquarters. After he had been introduced and they got down to business, the Norwegians showed him on a map a farmhouse they wanted shelled by the howitzer. It was located in a position commanding a road, the railway and a river valley. The Germans had about fifty paratroopers in there, according to the Norwegians, and they had some Norwegian prisoners, too..

c

So it was back to the station and the train for Salter. The engine was still hooked up and ready. They moved out.

They went to a position about 400 yards from the farmhouse, arriving at 2000 hours. Now the Norwegians were not quite sure where the Germans were. They opened fire on a small cottage 800 yards away. The light was still good, for this was the North, where the dusk came late. Salter began shelling the farmhouse just before dusk.

Of course he had no telephone system, so the firing was not easy. He ordered indirect fire to be carried out, giving his orders from an observation post on the hillside and passing them down a chain of men.

The gun was lashed down to the railway truck, but the springing interfered with the firing. Salter fired twenty rounds and decided the situation was not satisfactory, so that he stopped and they moved on back to the station to report to headquarters on the difficulties.

They decided on changing operations. Next morning they moved out early. Dawn came at 0300 hours and they wanted to get into action. They removed the gun from the truck and placed it on the track in a position to make direct fire possible.

The sixth shot fell close to the right of the target. The seventh and eighth were unobserved, but fell within the group of farm buildings on the hill, and the ninth and tenth were over and to the right.

The Norwegians moved in close to the farmhouse under cover of the firing, and after the tenth round they were close enough for the Norwegian commander to ask Salter to stop firing, lest they hit some Norwegian prisoners. The Germans surrendered then, and were taken prisoner by the Norwegians.

The railway was now clear for troops to move on down to Lillehammer, so that later that day the first British contingent, the Sherwood Foresters and Leicesters, passed through.

The forty-five German prisoners were taken to Dombas and Salter wondered at how young they seemed. None of them were more than eighteen by his reckoning.

At 1000 hours it was all over. Salter and his men replaced the howitzer on the truck and the train took them back to the town. There they remained. All day long the German planes came over. Sometimes they dived down and machine-gunned the town. But it was lackadaisical work, mostly from altitudes too high to cause any trouble.

Salter then had orders from Brigadier Morgan to remain where he was, so that he and his men settled in. All the next day there was sporadic machine-gunning, but oddly enough the German planes that kept flying over did not drop any bombs at all. That was Saturday.

On Sunday life changed. Bombing began, and very shortly after it had started a bomb exploded at the mouth of the station tunnel where the *Hood* men were dossed down. Seamen Harris and Kelly were wounded. Shrapnel caught Harris in the stomach and ripped into Kelly's lung. Able Seaman Walker's hand was fractured and there were five other minor injuries.

Hood's men were lucky, however. Five others in the tunnel were killed, including the American military attaché who was on hand that day.

Harris, Kelly and one other badly wounded man were taken out of the station when the bombing stopped and were moved to the Red Cross post outside the town. There they were cared for all day until a train picked them up and took them to hospital at Opdal.

That night, after the bombing, Sub-Lieutenant Salter tried to telephone the lieutenant-commander at Andalsnes, but the lines were down and he could not get through. Next morning, before he could try, he was given new orders by Colonel Simpson. He was to stay where he was and wait for replacements for the men he had lost.

Monday was a hard day, for the bombing continued all day long and they were forced to keep under cover. That afternoon Salter conferred with Admiral Sir Edward Evans who came to the hotel. The admiral suggested that they move the gun and the men down to Dovje which had not yet been bombed. They did so as soon as the railway line was repaired, and arrived there early on Tuesday morning. Conditions were even worse in Dovje. The Germans seemed to know the gun had come there; they bombed and strafed all day Tuesday. In the evening Salter decided to move back to Dombas and then over to the other side to the little town of Lesja, because where he was it was impossible to communicate with Andalsnes.

They moved that night and arrived at Lesja early next morning, Wednesday, 24 April. Once again Salter tried to get through to his command, but he was unable to make contact. He kept trying, although the Germans bombed and machine-gunned them all day from the air. The men sheltered in the woods and no one was hurt.

That night a despatch-rider found them and gave them orders to return to Andalsnes. They began the trip very early next morning when the line was repaired arriving at 0800 hours with the field gun and remaining ammunition. They had just about run out of food by that time.

All this while, Lieutenant Commander Awdry and the rest of the men of *Hood*'s naval contingent had been under almost constant bombardment during daylight hours.

Each day the bombing seemed to grow more intense. It became necessary to suspend operations at the port. Nothing could be moved during daylight hours without the certainty of being bombed. By the time Salter came back there was only one house left standing in the town. Yet because the men of *Hood* and the other ships were able to hide in the woods or to take cover in dug-outs, there were very few casualties.

By this time the place was a milling mass of refugees with troops and naval vessels delivering supplies. The machine-gunning was a constant harassment, but not as dangerous as the bombing, because the Germans for some reason never came down low enough to strafe successfully.

A few hours after young Salter came back with his men, Captain Champness arrived from the fleet to take command of the naval operations. But the end was already nearly in sight. Five days later, on 29 April, the captain ordered the men of *Hood* to get ready to embark. They were evacuating that evening.

It was all very secretive. The Norwegians were not to know about the British departure, because the place was by this time considered to be a nest of spies. What else could be expected with refugees coming from everywhere? Who could check papers when there were no papers?

Lieutenant-Commander Awdry kept a diplomatic silence until evening. Then he divided his men into working parties and sent them down to the quay independently, telling each party to meet him at 2100 hours.

The bombing was intense, and was very heavy that night on the quay. Seaman Thorpe was wounded in the leg. The story had been that a cruiser was coming in that night to take them off but it was a destroyer that came in, so that Awdry was only allowed to board fifteen men. He sent the crew of the howitzer and the wounded Thorpe.

Hood's contingent then lost all semblance of military unity. The camp and town were demolished already and that day they had been fired on continuously. Awdry could do nothing but tell the men to take to the woods at dawn and to meet him once more on the quay at 2330 hours the following night. So they had become, in a sense, guerrillas.

There was reason for the caution. Next day the whole camp was blown sky high and with it what remained of their personal belongings. They were also in serious danger of capture by this time, because the British plan had fallen apart for reasons beyond their control.

On 29 April they were almost totally disorganized and shifting for themselves. Some of them joined up with ratings from *Nelson* and walked twenty miles to Afaianes, where destroyers were being sent to pick up the stranded British fighters.

But the main body remained with Lieutenant-Commander Awdry and their patience was rewarded. At 2330 hours they were taken aboard the *Galatea* and were heading for Scapa Flow. Once there they were taken aboard *Rodney* and treated like kings. Finally they boarded a troopship which took them to Greenock. From there they travelled to Devonport and to *Hood* by 5 May. She was still in dock, still under repairs.

As for the other men of *Hood*, they had varied experiences One unit, with 4-inch guns, was sent to Alesund to set up the guns and protect the area. They arrived at 1500 hours on 18 April to be greeted by shouting and cheering Norwegians. The troops were billeted in the Norvoy and Klipra schools, and the officers went out to check on sites for the guns. They were accompanied by Captain Farstad and Captain Puntervold of the Norwegian forces.

Next day, Friday, the men began digging the gun sites. They put up machine-gun posts near Norvesundet bridge and established sentry posts with the Norwegians. They put up a signal station at Fjellstu on the heights. It was, so far, a proper naval operation.

Already, however, the British were in deep trouble all along the coast. The navy had no anti-aircraft batteries of any significance. On 19 April the Germans began their violent and destructive air attacks which met with almost no opposition at all. Hour after hour they were pasting the two ports of Andalsnes and Namsos.

Meanwhile, the German military machine, which had

stalled at the beginning, had gained time to recover and was starting its advance.

On Saturday, the twentieth, the naval units began putting up road blocks and machine-gun posts, in spite of repeated air attacks. HMS *Auckland* in the harbour managed to shoot down one plane around noon. But the bombing continued and there were a dozen air-raid alarms.

The bombing grew more severe and the men had their first indication that all was not well; they were ordered not to mount the 4-inch guns they were digging emplacements for. Everyone knew what that meant. That evening the *Auckland* sailed and that also was construed as a bad sign.

The raids subsided that night, but began again at 0300 hours. The objectives seemed to be oil storage tanks at Osenholmen, a steamer that was in dry dock at Breivik and the wireless telegraph station at Akala. There was a certain amount of machine-gunning too, but here as elsewhere, it did not seem to be very enthusiastic.

Although there were five raids that day, the men kept digging between times, but they made no attempt to mount the guns.

On Monday, 22 April, *St Magnus* arrived to coal, escorted by the warship *Javelin*. The German planes swarmed in to attack *Javelin*, but did not succeed in doing any damage. One small Norwegian freighter on the fjord north of the town was attacked and set on fire. The raids were worse, almost continual from 0700 to 1700 hours.

The seriousness of the situation became apparent when it was announced that the town was to be placed under military control.

On Tuesday, 23 April, there was promise of anti-aircraft guns and ammunition to protect the area from these cease-less attacks. The bombing continued.

Next day two anti-aircraft guns, and 1,000 rounds of ammunition were landed early in the morning. The bombing had stopped, but somehow this seemed more ominous than not. Soon enough, the men here would have the same experiences as those elsewhere in Norway.

Lieutenant E. D. Strand of the Royal Marines, who had become separated from the naval contingent on arrival at Andalsnes reported to Colonel H. W. Simpson and was instructed to proceed to Lesjeskog where there was a lake. The plan called for a squadron of Gladiators to fly off the carriers; for the marines to defend the frozen lake on which they would operate, and in particular the petrol supply. Strand was to move on up to the lake and there report to Wing Commander Keen of the RAF.

The marines were to set out by train. But the bombers were ahead of them and they had knocked out the line, so that they returned to Andalsnes and waited. Motor transport was arranged and soon they were on their way again.

The RAF party consisted of about thirty ground staff personnel, two Oerlikon gun crews under Sub-Lieutenant Goodale of the Navy, and one platoon of Royal Marines. The mixed bag indicated the entire nature of the Norwegian operation, assembled in haste, and directed in a hurry.

They all arrived at the lake about 1700 hours on 22 April, and were billeted in an old school about a mile from the petrol dump and flying field.

That night the petrol came in, and was hidden in small amounts in the woods adjoining the field. Next morning the platoon took up positions around the area and dug in.

Lieutenant Strand set up patrols. One platoon was always patrolling the dump, and at night another was sleeping by the dump, because the billet was too far from the area to be of any use in case of emergency.

Thus only one platoon had a good night's sleep in the billets, but that was more than anyone expected.

As for the others, they tramped about in the snow and felt frozen. Those trying to sleep in the woods near the dump found that impossible. The cold was too bitter in the un-heated huts they occupied.

On the evening of 23 April, the Gladiator squadron arrived on the frozen lake, followed by another squadron that was completely unexpected.

The Germans had been visiting. They came over on the twenty-third but just for a look. As if they knew the planes were on the way, they waited until the morning of the twenty-fourth and then began bombing furiously. They bombed so heavily that the men wondered how much use they could be.

They found out at 1700 hours when the orders came to evacuate the position.

That afternoon the marines had got hold of some Lewis guns, and they fitted them up and began firing at the Germans if they came in low enough. But the Lewis guns did not turn the tide. The orders stood, and they prepared to move out.

Soon enough the Marines were moved to other areas for fighting duty. The retreat was on and they would have to cover it. By 1 May Lieutenant Strand found himself in command of a force that consisted of two marine platoons, one from *Hood* and the other from *Nelson*, and a platoon from the Green Howards. His orders were to hold a position south of Verma until 2130 hours. It was an important moment in the desperate withdrawal of the British, which was fast becoming a rout. He got into position at 1600 hours with the two Royal Marine platoons forward and the army platoon in reserve.

Hood's men were on the right under Sergeant J. P. Lees. They had the job of covering the road block in the vicinity, and the slopes of the valley on their right. *Nelson*'s Royal Marines were on the left and their task was similar: to cover the road block on the railway and the slope of the hill to the left. The army platoon was in position around the third road block.

Strand had been told that an encounter with the Germans was most unlikely here, since the road in front which ran between Verma and Dombas had been made impassable at many points. So the Germans would almost certainly not be coming his way, and his task was really only to look out for air attackers.

Following these instructions Strand had few men on watch. The cover was scant and the danger to them would be tremendous if the Germans came in bombing and strafing as he had already known them to do at the airfield on the lake.

It was quiet. *Nelson*'s platoon had one section on watch on the road block, and a Lewis machine-gun covering the valley. The remainder of the forward platoons were under cover about 150 yards behind the forward position.

At 1755 a runner came back to the command post to sound the alarm. Something was up. Men were running everywhere. Lieutenant Strand started forward to discover what was happening. He got about fifty yards ahead and saw several men running back around a bend in the road. He sent the runner back to see what that was all about and went on. He told the runner that the sergeant in charge should bring the men back. Then he went on.

The runner did not come back. After ten minutes or so, the lieutenant sent another man to find the first. Another ten minutes went by. No one appeared. Puzzled to exasperation, Lieutenant Strand headed back to the bend himself.

Not a man was in sight. The place was eerie with quiet. He hurried back to the last road block and there he found a small party of the army platoon under a sergeant. Altogether there were only four men in the group.

They said that a large number of soldiers had come rushing down the hill shouting that all was lost, and that the Germans were just behind them, and that most of the platoon had panicked, joined them, and gone off in the lorries belonging to the defence force. Lieutenant Strand thanked them and went off to look for his lorries. Sure enough, when he got to the park, he found that they were gone and so were the men.

He rousted about and collected all the men he could find. He found Corporal Butler and Marine Swatton from the *Nelson*, and Marines McPherson and Lashmar from the *Hood*. Together they took up the position they had been assigned and held it until 2330 hours. He sent the army sergeant and Marine Welch from *Hood* back to headquarters with a report. Finally he, too, was recalled.

The Norwegian adventure was virtually finished.

7

Encounter with the French

Hood's refit was a long time happening, or so it seemed. She was not ready for sea again until nearly the end of May. In that period a thousand years had gone by in terms of change, for Britain, seemingly at stalemate that spring, had become a beleaguered island since the fall of the French armies and the disastrous retreat to the beaches of Dunkirk.

There was no place for Hood at Dunkirk. She was heading for Liverpool and the last bit of tidying up to complete her refit. It was 12 June before she was ready for action once more. Her companion ships had been busy all this while, some even bringing back the remnants from Norway, which was a disaster all round.

But late on the afternoon of 12 June *Hood* sailed out of Liverpool bound for the convoy US 3 heading for the Clyde. She would escort them in and make sure they were safe so far.

She was out for four days, and arrived at Greenock on the sixteenth with the convoy safe and sound. Two days later she sailed for Gibraltar.

At this point the men were told what was going to happen: *Hood* was going south to rendezvous with *Ark Royal*, and the pair, battleship and carrier, were to proceed to the Rock, and there form the nucleus of the new force that would be called Force H.

Admiral Dönitz was giving Britain a good deal of trouble in the Mediterranean and Whitehall had decided that the convoy routes between Gibraltar and Sierra

Leone needed a powerful independent force, which could operate in the western Mediterranean without throwing the fleet all askew.

Vice-Admiral Sir James Somerville would fly his flag of command in *Hood*. They would report directly to London, and not to Sir Dudley North, commander of the North Atlantic station, who was based at Gibraltar. They were to be truly independent. The Admiralty had the idea there would be plenty for them to do.

Hood was detached on 18 June, and headed south. The weather was warm and sunny in the Bay of Biscay and right on schedule they sighted *Ark Royal*, her flight deck lifting and swaying in the long swell of the open Atlantic. They steamed in consort, the planes of the carrier protecting them from unpleasant surprises from submarines, and they reached the Rock on the twenty-third.

There was shore leave, as there almost always was at Gibraltar, and care was taken to see that the men had as much of it as could be managed. There were indications that something was afoot. What that something was, of course, was very military, very political. With the fall of France, something had to be done about the French fleet in the Mediterranean. In Allied hands it could be valuable asset in the war against the Axis powers. In Axis hands it could bring disaster.

There was one fine week at Gibraltar, and then the action began.

The task of Force H was specifically to secure the transfer, surrender or destruction of the French warships at Oran and Mers-el-Kebir, lest they fall into the hands of the Germans or Italians. The orders were precise and admitted very little latitude.

This was all made plain to Admiral Somerville on the afternoon of 27 June when he was called to Whitehall to meet with the First Sea Lord and the First Lord of the Admiralty.

Later in the day they had a more informal discussion, and the Admiralty officials told Somerville they hoped it would not be necessary to use force, although of course they must be prepared for it.

After this meeting Somerville was of the opinion that the French collapse was so complete and their will to fight so totally extinguished that no one in London really believed there would be any trouble in taking over the ships.

On 28 June, then, at 1300 hours, the admiral and his staff boarded HMS *Arethusa* at Spithead, and hastened to Gibraltar to meet *Hood*.

All the way south the air-waves hummed with messages about the proposed operation. The possibility of Spain's entry into the war on the Axis side was considered.

Somerville learned that his opposite number, Admiral Cunningham of the Mediterranean Fleet, was very much opposed to the use of force to take the French ships either at Alexandria or at Oran.

On 30 June, when the *Arethusa* arrived at Gibraltar at 1745 hours, Admiral Somerville hurried to see Admiral Sir Dudley North, commander of the North Atlantic station, and discuss the matter with him.

He found North, too, was opposed to the use of force and felt it should be avoided at all costs. That evening Somerville called a meeting of his senior officers to discuss the Oran operation. Admiral Wells, commander of the carriers, said he thought a torpedo-attack by planes would be difficult and unproductive unless the anti-aircraft guns at Oran were silenced first.

It was finally decided that at Mers-el-Kebir a round or two should be fired followed by a limited firing to cause evacuation of the ships. No one wanted to move into Oran with gun-fire in view of the number of civilian casualties that would be the result of such a move.

When the meeting was over, Admiral North, Vice-

Admiral Wells and Captain A. S. Holland all expressed once again their opposition to the use of force. They did not believe there was any reason to fear that the French would allow their ships to fall into German hands.

Holland's opinion was important, because he had had more association with the French over a longer period of time than anyone else in the area. He was to be the emissary of Somerville and the Admiralty in this delicate mission to the French.

North suggested that Somerville should not listen just to these senior officers, but that he have a talk with Lieutenant-Commander A. Y. Spearman and Lieutenant-Commander G. B. S. Davies, who had both been in close liaison with French naval authorities recently. They too said that the use of force should be avoided if possible, because it would be bound to alienate them and transform them from a defeated ally into an active enemy.

Somerville was impressed by the arguments. He despatched a message to London suggesting that the plan be changed. But London was obdurate. Either the French would join up, turn over their ships or the ships must be destroyed. His suggestions were not acceptable.

Somerville was still not convinced that 'Their Lordships' in London knew what they were about. For those on the spot who knew the French were unanimous in the opinion that to follow this course would be disastrous. Yet as he considered the situation, he did not really expect the French to fight. 'At the worst,' he said, 'they might fire a few token shots before abandoning their ships.'

On 2 July, therefore, it was all settled and he, as commander, had made the best of it. He held another meeting of senior officers in the morning, and discussed the orders for Operation Catapult.

What they had been waiting for, which the men did not know, was the coming of the battleship *Valiant*. She arrived on 2 July and Admiral Somerville was eager to be off.

Hood was flying Somerville's flag and *Ark Royal* that of Vice-Admiral L. V. Wells. Also in the force were *Valiant*, *Resolution*, the light cruisers *Arethusa* and *Enterprise* and two flotillas of destroyers, eleven in all.

At 1400 hours on 2 July the force set sail. It was imperative that the French be flushed out and made to make the decisions about the future.

The ring was closing. Already, a few days earlier, *Hood* and *Ark Royal* had made one brief sortie to intercept the French battleship *Richelieu* and force her into Gibraltar. In fact they did not. She was met elsewhere by the cruiser *Dorsetshire* and taken into port in Dakar.

In London the War Cabinet was edgy. Winston Churchill and the others wanted those French warships either in Allied hands or at the bottom of the sea, no middle course. The French ships that found themselves in British ports at this time were rudely boarded and taken over. At Alexandria, Admiral Godfrey was persuaded to stay by Admiral Cunningham, after long and painstaking negotiations.

But Admiral Gensoul at Oran was a different man. He was proud in the Gallic manner. The suspicion of England was strong in him and what was happening elsewhere did nothing to allay it.

That was what concerned Admiral Somerville this July day. His orders were to take or destroy the French ships.

No one seemed conscious of the supreme irony of it. *Hood* was now to lead the force that would go after the admiral who had led them out not so very many months ago on a mission against a common enemy. *Hood* had then taken station on *Dunkerque*, now she was to take aim at the self-same ship and the admiral who had once, in a sense, commanded the big battleship was now to feel something completely different.

Operation Catapult began on the afternoon of 2 July.

The name 'Hood' derived from a distinguished line of British seamen. The third *Hood*, pictured here in 1893 (above) and 1904 (below), was launched in 1891, changed her appearance at the turn of the century, and went out gallantly in 1914 blocking the entrance to Portland Harbour against German U-boat torpedoes.

HMS *Hood:* The last of a line of ships to bear the name, *Hood* was the
mightiest ship afloat and symbolized British sea power between the wars.
Seen here at anchor in 1933, and (below left and right) amidships details.
In the design special emphasis was placed on the protection of the magazines,
but this proved inadequate to meet the rigours of modern warfare.

SMS *Bismarck* was one of the last in the long, and always formidable, line of German Dreadnoughts, and was built to a size far exceeding the agreements in any naval treaty. Seen here (left) at the jubilant scene of her launching at Hamburg in 1939 in the presence of the highest Nazi officials; (middle) at sea in 1941 at the start of her last mission; and (bottom) *Bismarck*'s eight 15-inch guns were more modern than *Hood*'s.

On *Hood*'s doomed encounter with *Bismarck* she was accompanied by *Prince of Wales* (above), who still carried dockyard civilians on board. She survived the ordeal, only to be sunk by five torpedoes later in the same year. *Prinz Eugen* (below) was an Austrian Dreadnought, neat, compact and powerful. Similar in design to *Bismarck*, she seemed like a small shadow sailing beside her.

Through a mix-up, *Ark Royal* was not included on the orders, and this error created more than a little confusion before it was sorted out.

The destroyers left first to carry out an anti-submarine sweep of the approaches and Gibraltar bay. The orders began to go out and the submarine *Proteus* was informed that Force H was going to be operating off Oran as of 0600 hours of 3 July. She was to patrol well clear of this area.

The force sailed at 0500 hours. They took formation, zig-zagging at 17 knots until 2130 hours when they slowed down and stopped the zigzag pattern. They were heading for Oran and her port, Mers-el-Kebir, the naval base just west of the city.

One of the key people in the mission was Captain C. S. Holland. He was charged with the task of the actual physical meeting with the French.

At 2200 hours this first night, Admiral Somerville informed Captain Holland that the Admiralty had told him the French had a scheme for the 'demilitarization' of their ships, and this was supposed to work on two hours' notice. The admiral told the captain to be certain to find out about this, to make sure it was real and workable. What the British needed to know was whether the proposed measures would keep the ships from service for at least twelve months, even in dockyards.

Holland was riding in the destroyer *Foxhound*, which would be expected to negotiate the entrance and enter the harbour. Holland would then present the British demands to Admiral Gensoul in the *Dunkerque*, while Somerville and his ships lay just outside.

At 2347 hours the force had something of a scare. A torpedo exploded ahead of the destroyer *Vortigern*. She swung immediately into action with the destroyer *Vidette*. They spent more than an hour in search of the offending U-boat, but found nothing.

Back in London the cabinet grew even more nervous. A signal came in at 0130 hours that morning. London was not setting a time limit on the acceptance of the demands, but it was of the utmost importance that the mission be completed during the daylight hours of 3 July.

No time limit? That seemed like a time limit indeed. Another hour and a half went by. Needless to say Admiral Somerville was on his feet.

At 0300 hours he despatched *Foxhound* to go on ahead and deliver Captain Holland to the *Dunkerque*. Communication was established with the port war-signal station, and permission was asked for the ship to enter port.

At 0620 another message was sent, this one to Admiral Gensoul:

Adresse à Amiral Gensoul

L'Amirante Britannique envoie le commandant Holland conferer avec vous. La Marine Royale espère que les propositions vont vous permettre, la Marine Nationale Française vaillante et glorieuse, de se ranger à nos côtes. En ce cas vos batiments resteraient toujours les votres et personne, n'aurait besoin d'aucun anxiète dans l'avenir.

La Flotte Britannique est au large d'Oran pour vous acuellir.

'*Vaillante et glorieuse*' – how much good would that do to cover the steel fist with the velvet glove? Soon enough, Holland would see, and then the admiral would know.

8

Oran

HMS *Foxhound* received permission to enter the harbour at Mers-el Kebir at 0742 hours, and ten minutes later the pilot boat came skimming up. The French pilot came aboard to announce that *Foxhound* was to go inside and berth near the flagship *Dunkerque*.

Admiral Somerville was not going to accept that. Captain Holland was going inside as an emissary and he was risking a good deal personally in so doing, although he had confidence in the honour of the French.

To put one of His Majesty's warships into a possible trap, for it to be made a hostage, was more than Somerville cared to risk. Therefore, pleading the need to keep in touch closely with the commanding officer of Force H, the captain of the destroyer anchored outside the anti-submarine net about a mile and a half from Mers-el-Kebir lighthouse.

The destroyer was at anchor a few minutes after 0800 hours. Almost at that moment the Admiral's barge came alongside and a French officer announced that the admiral was unable to see the English representative, but that the chief of staff would see him. The bearer of this message was the admiral's flag-lieutenant, so that Captain Holland knew it was official enough.

Holland was considering the next course of action, when a signal came to *Foxhound* from Force H. She was to sail immediately. Obviously, something was up.

A reconnaissance aircraft had been flown off *Ark Royal* and had been moving about overhead since 0630 hours. In the beginning, the French fleet anchorage had appeared normal enough: the big ships with their awnings spread, the silence of a harbour at rest. But at 0830, after the arrival of the *Foxhound* at the end of the harbour, the French battle-ships and cruisers seemed to be getting up steam. They were also furling awnings.

Swiftly, Captain Holland and Lieutenant-Commander A. Y. Spearman, the former British naval liaison officer at Bizerta, embarked in *Foxhound*'s motor-boat and cast off. All hands were summoned on deck and *Foxhound* weighed anchor and headed out to join the fleet.

Shortly after 2100 hours, Admiral Somerville moved Force H nearer Oran. Paravanes were streaming as they were taking no chances on mines, but the ships' guns were trained fore and aft, a sign that they did not come in war.

They were there, just off the breakwater and could see the upper works of the French ships clearly. Visibility was at least six miles that morning. Admiral Somerville waited.

Meanwhile, Captain Holland was met halfway between the inner boom and the breakwater by the barge of Admiral Gensoul. Once again the flag-lieutenant was on board.

Aboard the big ships outside the signalmen were sending the message in French:

I am sending Captain Holland to confer with you. The Royal Navy hopes that the proposals made will allow the valiant and glorious French Navy to range itself on our side. In this case your ships will remain in your hands and no one need have any fear for the future. The British fleet is lying off Oran to welcome you. . . .

Since the admiral would not see him, Captain Holland decided to hand over to the flag-lieutenant the instructions he carried. These offered Admiral Gensoul four choices:

1. He could put to sea, join the British and fight against Hitler and Mussolini.

2. He could sail (with reduced crews) to a British port for internment, or later decision about the future.

3. He could put to sea with reduced crews and sail to a French West Indies port (if he felt he could not break the armistice with the Germans and Italians).

4. He could scuttle his ships within six hours.

If none of these ideas appealed to Admiral Gensoul? 'I have the orders of His Majesty's government', Admiral Somerville had written, 'to use whatever force may be necessary to prevent your ships from falling into German or Italian hands.'

There was one final alternative. Somerville had heard that the French had some method of speedy demilitarization of their ships, and if Admiral Gensoul wished to take that course, he could do so, provided the British had a guarantee that it could be done within six hours, and that the fleet would be laid up for at least a year.

As the admiral's barge pulled up alongside Captain Holland's motor-boat, the flag-lieutenant indicated that it might be very difficult for the chief of staff to see Captain Holland at once.

Holland considered sending in Lieutenant-Commander Spearman, but then he decided to send the British proposals, as he called them – the French called them 'ultimatum' – to the chief of staff via the flag-lieutenant. He handed them over and said he would wait for a reply. He then sent a message to Admiral Somerville warning that the French were avoiding him.

When the British 'ultimatum' arrived, the chief of staff rushed it in to Admiral Gensoul. He took a few moments to digest what he read, and then sent a message to the French Admiralty. His digest was simple enough: the British had threatened that unless he scuttled his ships in six hours they would attack him. To this his reply was: 'French ships will meet force with force.'

At around 2200 hours the flag-lieutenant returned to Captain Holland in the harbour and gave him a written reply which said that much. However, it did say also that the French ships would not be allowed to fall into the hands of the Germans.

Captain Holland and the French flag-lieutenant held a friendly conversation, and at the end of it Holland sent to the chief of staff a personal note together with a previously prepared message. The flag-lieutenant took them in.

This time the chief of staff came out to meet with Holland, bringing a written reply, which reiterated everything that had been said already. In other words, if the British fired a single round at the French fleet inside, it would alienate every Frenchman, every French naval officer and every French rating. So it was impasse. Captain Holland returned to *Foxhound* about half an hour before noon.

All this while, Admiral Somerville had led Force H back and forth across the mouth of the bay, moving out to sea a bit and then back in again. *Ark Royal* was detached to go off and recover her aircraft in the wind. They had flown a protective screen about the force, while observation planes checked the French ships and reported on their movements.

The level of activity had been increasing all day. The destroyers had long since furled their awnings, the *Paris* was hoisting in her boats about noon, and it was apparent that they were all preparing to go to sea.

The admiral instructed the carrier to watch through those aerial eyes for submarines in the waters off Oran, but not one was yet spotted.

When Captain Holland reached *Foxhound*, he discovered a message from Admiral Somerville waiting for him. The French must understand, said the admiral, that he was not going to allow them to leave the harbour unless they accepted his terms. Holland decided to send this message with

Lieutenant-Commander Spearman and the flag-lieutenant had it before noon.

Meanwhile Somerville received some good news from Alexandria, where French Admiral Godfrey had chosen to demilitarize his ships in harbour rather than quarrel with his English hosts. The flagship began blinking off that message to the *Dunkerque*.

Foxhound now moved outside the outer boom to be away from harm in case it all came to shooting. As she came out, her wireless operator sent a message to *Hood* which summarized Admiral Gensoul's replies to Somerville's demands. It seemed obvious from these words that the French were going to put to sea and fight. Admiral Somerville therefore decided to mine the entrance to the port.

He gave the orders. He also sent a message to Whitehall: he was prepared to open fire at 1330 hours that same afternoon. At about that time Admiral Somerville asked Captain Holland if he saw any alternative to opening fire with the main batteries. Captain Holland replied that he was hoping that the French might accept the 'proposals' before the expiration of the time limit.

The way Holland put it aroused some doubts in the admiral as to what precisely the captain had said to the chief of staff.

'Does anything you have said prevent me from opening fire?' he asked.

Holland replied that the use of force might be avoided if *Foxhound* went in close enough for visual signalling, and asked if there was any further message from the French. The admiral thought that over.

He had instructed *Ark Royal* to mine the harbour, and the carrier had flown off minelaying aircraft at a few minutes after 1300 hours. Five mines were laid directly in the entrance to Mers-el-Kebir. Apparently the French noticed, because the boom, which had been opened, was closed shortly afterwards and there was other activity inside the harbour which indicated that the French knew what was happening. They seemed to have stopped their preparations to leave.

The admiral decided he would wait until 1500 hours for the French to make up their minds. About half an hour later, as *Foxhound* was moving in closer to *Dunkerque*, one of the *Ark Royal* aircraft announced that submarines could be seen leaving Oran.

Admiral Somerville now issued swift orders. *Vortigern* was to be detached immediately and proceed to the entrance of Oran harbour, to stop and if necessary to sink any submarine attempting to leave. *Ark Royal* was told that her aircraft were to do the same.

It was a false alarm, however. A few minutes later came a second report. The submarines were simply shifting their positions, and instead of heading for sea they seemed to be seeking additional protection from the mole.

Admiral Somerville was really hoping the French would accept the terms. He now told *Foxhound* to instruct Admiral Gensoul to hoist a large square flag at the mast-head if he accepted the terms. He waited again.

He felt he had waited as long as possible, and was prepared for one final message when word came from the French flagship. Admiral Gensoul was willing to receive a delegate for 'honourable discussion'.

So it was back inside for Captain Holland. Accompanied by Lieutenant-Commander Davies, he got back into the *Foxhound*'s motor-boat and headed in.

Admiral Somerville was not quite sure what it was all about; he wondered if the French were stalling for time, or if Admiral Gensoul had only now realized how determined the British were and that it would be a matter of using force.

As the harbour was now closed by mines, *Foxhound* could

not put in too close to discharge Captain Holland, and so he had to make a journey of seven and a half miles inshore by motor-boat. It took a bit of time.

The ceremonies of arrival at the French flagship took more, and so it was 1615 hours before Holland arrived at the barge.

The captain had noticed coming in how the French ships were now almost ready to put to sea. He also gathered that the admiral had sent a message through the fleet. For as his motor-boat came by and as he transferred to the barge, the men on the decks of the ships stood to attention.

As he passed through the battle-cruisers, he saw that all the control positions were manned, and that tugs with steam up were standing by the sterns of each ship. The French were ready to do something.

Captain Holland, having reached the deck of *Dunkerque*, was escorted with all civility to the admiral's cabin. As he entered, Admiral Gensoul was most cordial to him. The admiral could not keep the indignation from his voice when he spoke about the ultimatum and the mining of the harbour by his – 'allies'.

They talked. The admiral produced secret orders from Admiral Darlan, dated 24 June. He assured the captain that he would never allow his ships to fall into the hands of the Germans.

But that was not enough. Captain Holland had to tell him that the British government meant what was said in those various alternative proposals. The discussion was lengthy, and it seemed to take a long time for the admiral to be finally convinced that Force H would actually attack him unless he met the conditions.

Outside the gunners of the big ships were ready. The range-takers were at work constantly keeping the gunners informed. The big ships roamed back and forth, easily, nervously.

At about 1615, Admiral Somerville received a message from the Admiralty that hastened affairs. He was to settle matters quickly or reinforcements would be sent. The French had received Gensoul's original signal and had ordered all French vessels within striking distance of Oran to go to his assistance. That might mean French submarines, and it was a possibility Somerville was not eager to contemplate.

In the meantime aircraft had been flown again and two more mines laid, this time in front of Oran harbour.

Admiral Somerville wasted no time. He prepared a signal, which was passed to Admiral Gensoul immediately. At the same time the word went out to Force H. 'Prepare for ANVIL at 1730.' The first shots were to be fired at 1730 hours.

Holland was doing the very best he could to assuage French pride and to achieve the ends of the Admiralty. On receipt of this message, he wrote out a message in reply, showed it to Admiral Gensoul, and the French wireless operators despatched it.

The French crews were being reduced, said Holland, and the ships were ready to proceed to Martinique or the United States if threatened by the enemy. The message was received at 1729, a minute before the deadline, and the admiral pondered it.

But this message did not fulfil any of the conditions laid down by the Admiralty in the original proposals. Admiral Somerville had no right to accept this offer.

He gave the order for *Ark Royal* to fly off her planes and for the battleships to move in towards the coast. The turrets turned and the guns began to lift. Still Admiral Somerville delayed, but this time it was not from any indecision; he was waiting for Captain Holland.

Holland left the deck of the French flagship at 1725 hours, and as he was piped over the side, he heard the call to action stations aboard the French vessels. The admiral's barge took him out to his motor-boat, and there he transferred, and headed for the harbour entrance. It was already after 1730, but the admiral wanted his emissary clear before the action began.

Holland was clear at 1754, and Somerville ordered his ships to fire on their old ally. The range was 17,500 yards and the line of fire was from the northwest, with the aircraft from *Ark Royal* spotting for them.

The guns of the *Hood*, those 15-inch guns, began to boom. At the same time an aircraft report was received from one of *Ark Royal*'s planes. The French destroyers inside the harbour were beginning to move inside the boom.

Three minutes after the British guns began to fire there came a huge explosion inside the harbour, followed by a volume of smoke that rose several hundred feet into the air. A shell had struck the magazines of the battleship *Bretagne*. She went dead in the water and burned hotly.

Almost immediately another smaller explosion was seen and heard offshore. One of the French destroyers had blown up. By this time, so many hits had been registered on so many ships that the harbour was filled with smoke and flame, and visual spotting of the salvoes was no longer possible. Even air spotting was not satisfactory.

The enemy shore batteries were firing merrily. *Arethusa* engaged them, and *Enterprise* tried, but her guns did not have the range. The French were shooting well, and soon heavy projectiles began to fall around the British battleships. They were, said the watchers, 13·4-inch shells, and they were coming close, sometimes straddling.

After the British had fired thirty-six 15-inch salvoes, the French ships' fire slacked off, but the forts continued to fire away and their shooting was getting better all the time. The admiral altered course and ordered the ships to make smoke to protect themselves from the shore batteries.

The battleships stopped firing on the French at 1804.

The French ship fire was decreasing. Actually *Bretagne* was a burning hulk, the *Provence* was on fire and her captain had tried to beach her in shallow water to prevent her from sinking. The *Dunkerque* was crippled and on fire, and the rest seemed to be equally badly off.

The admiral felt that if he stopped firing, he could cut the loss of life, and perhaps persuade Admiral Gensoul to finally accept the British terms.

This sense of humanity gave the French an opportunity they had not expected. Admiral Somerville was confident that the French were trapped inside their harbour. He knew they were aware that the harbour entrance was mined and he felt quite sure that no attempt at escape would be made.

He did not understand the depth of the emotions that had seized the French when the British representatives had turned upon them so suddenly. Whatever friendliness had been engendered in years of association was wiped out and replaced in many cases by blind hatred. But more than that was the feeling of pride in the French, that they must do for themselves what would be done. The British had given them a mortal insult in refusing to accept their statement that they would never allow their ships to fall into Hitler's hands.

They meant it, that much was sure. The British might comfort themselves by saying the French did not know how they might have been set upon by Hitler, denied the resources to get to the Americas, sunk even by Dönitz's u-boats. But to the French these arguments added up to nothing.

Those ships that could fight, therefore, were determined to get away from this trap, if they possibly could.

9

Escape

At 1804 hours when Admiral Somerville ordered the ships of Force H to stop firing on the French, he did so with considerable relief. It was not very pleasant for an officer schooled in the traditions of the Royal Navy to shoot sitting ducks, and he ended it as soon as he felt he could.

Force H then proceeded to move west, for the admiral wanted to take a position where further bombardment could be effected if it seemed necessary, without either causing casualties among Frenchmen moving ashore in boats, or exposing the ships of the force to the fire of the forts. They had tried to be careful earlier to avoid hitting any buildings or causing any civilian casualties.

The admiral had another reason for moving west. Earlier in the afternoon he had learned that there was some activity at the French military airfield outside Oran. As there was now a thick cloud of smoke lying between the ships and the shore, he could not rule out the possibility of unfriendly French aircraft coming out of the smoke and making a very swift and possibly effective attack on his ships. To avoid this, the westward move was wise.

As it was he thought he might have to resume the unfortunate shelling of the French ships, because he did not see what he wanted, evidence of compliance with his government's orders.

From the shore came the messages again: 'Please cease fire.' Back to the shore went the message:

'Unless I see your ships sinking, I shall open fire again.'

That is how matters stood late in the afternoon, with the dusk closing in.

A quarter of an hour after the *Hood* and the others had stopped firing, Admiral Somerville had a message from one of *Ark Royal's* aircraft.

One vessel of the *Dunkerque* class was leaving harbour, heading east.

The admiral simply did not believe the report. Earlier in the day he had received others about the movement inside the harbour, and when he had responded to them, he had discovered that they were not meaningful. Besides, he was now certain that the French would abandon their ships. He knew the smoke pall above the harbour was such that it could play tricks with the eyes of observers. So he did nothing.

Meanwhile, the battle-cruiser *Strasbourg*, with five destroyers around her, had indeed threaded its way out of the harbour, avoided the mines, and was bent on escape.

The admiral was tidying up. He learned that in the straddling of *Hood* by the gunfire from the forts, one officer and one rating had been hit by shell splinters. Two wounded, however, seemed little enough a price to pay for the success of the action he had just gone through.

But ten minutes later, the *Ark Royal* aircraft's report was confirmed by another. The battle-cruiser and several destroyers had definitely been sighted, outside the harbour, moving rapidly eastwards.

The admiral had already decided he must take stronger action against the ships in Mers-el-Kebir, and had ordered Admiral Wells to fly off six Swordfish with armour-piercing bombs to attack the battle-cruisers in the harbour. They were delayed because of the necessity of recovering other aircraft, and so it was 1825 before they began taking off. They were accompanied by Skuas for protection.

When the second report came in, however, these aircraft

were in the air and heading for the harbour, so that the admiral ordered them to be diverted to search for the escaping battle-cruiser and the destroyers.

Admiral Somerville himself was diverted again, this time by the destroyer *Wrestler*, which had been ordered to stand by at the entrance to the Oran harbour and ensure that no ships went in or out. She was being engaged by a shore-battery, her captain reported, and the salvoes were coming close.

Admiral Somerville ordered the destroyer to retire out of range. It was just in time, for the enemy were getting warmed up, and a hundred 4- and 6-inch shells fell around her before she escaped, luckily unharmed.

The time flew. It was 1843 before the cruisers and the destroyers were ordered to move up and take after the fleeing French ships. The reports were confusing. Admiral Somerville did not know how many French ships had actually left the harbour. In a few minutes things sorted themselves out, air observation and intelligence reports made sense: the one battle-cruiser was out with several destroyers.

That being the case, Admiral Somerville ordered *Hood* and her destroyers to set after them. The remainder of the force was to be left behind to continue its guard duty. It was to follow on later without a screen.

In the air, the bombers moved towards the French force. As they approached and prepared to attack they ran into heavy and accurate anti-aircraft fire. One Swordfish fell, and then another.

The bombs were dropping but the French warships took evasive action. However, the pilots on their return said they believed one hit had been made with a 250-pound bomb, but not enough damage had been done to make any serious claims. The French were getting away.

It was not too long before *Hood* and her destroyers

arrived on the scene. *Strasbourg* and her destroyers were long gone, but the crews of the two Swordfish were there paddling about in the water. *Wrestler* picked them up.

All this while, Captain Holland and his assistants were speeding after *Hood*. Luckily the battle-cruiser had not reached full speed, so that they were able to catch up with her in their little motor-boat flying its big white ensign.

They were taken aboard as *Hood* steamed ahead; the captain, Lieutenant-Commander Spearman, Lieutenant-Commander Davies and the boat's crew. Holland then reported to the admiral and told him what had happened on board the French warship.

By 1920 hours *Hood* was up to full speed. Travelling with her were *Arethusa* and *Enterprise*, and ahead of her the destroyers. Eight minutes later, the look-outs spied a French destroyer moving west and close to the coast. *Arethusa* and *Enterprise* engaged her. *Hood* fired a few salvoes from those big 15-inch guns and *Valiant*, which had come up, also used her heavy armament.

Hits were observed, at least three of them, and then the destroyer turned back towards Oran, but not without a last defiant stab. As she turned away, look-outs in the tops of *Hood* spotted torpedoes approaching on the starboard bow.

Hood took evasive action and it was four minutes until the danger had passed and she resumed her base course.

It was nearing darkness, but at 1950 hours six more Swordfish were flown off *Ark Royal* with orders to press home an attack on the battle-cruiser.

The chase was on for certain now. *Hood* was travelling at top speed and the others were moving with her. But at 2020 the word came that *Strasbourg* and eleven destroyers were twenty-five miles ahead. They could not catch her in less than an hour even if she were to stop dead. From reports received during the afternoon and evening, Admiral Somerville calculated that the French force from Algiers, which included several cruisers with 8- and 6-inch guns and many destroyers, would be meeting *Strasbourg* at about 2100 hours.

He considered a night engagement, but the prospects of finding the battle-cruiser at night were not very good. Neither of his destroyer flotillas had much experience in night work and that made it worse.

The geography of the chase was against them. Force H would be silhouetted against the afterglow if they did find the enemy. That would make them good targets long before they could find the French. Furthermore, the speed of the chase would be such that the destroyers would have no time to spread out, and these v and w class destroyers did not have enough fuel left for more than a three-hour chase.

Under night conditions he was uncertain that *Hood* could keep up with the advance forces, and without her they would be at a distinct disadvantage if they met *Strasbourg*.

Considering all these facts, and the additional worry that *Valiant* and *Resolution* were moving along unscreened, and thus at the mercy of submarines and even possibly of enemy destroyers, the admiral decided against extending the pursuit. He did not believe that the possible loss of British ships at this point would be justified, even if the Germans did manage to acquire *Strasbourg*. British resources were very precious these days and every vessel counted.

The French would fight. There was no question about that. In fact they were already doing so. For as the admiral pondered, *Hood* and the other ships were fending off attacks by French bombers. Most of the bombs fell wide, but *Wrestler* suffered four near-misses from bombs that fell within fifty yards of her.

As for the air attack on the French battle-cruiser, it was proceeding as scheduled. The pilots found the French force just before 2100 hours, which was twenty minutes after sunset. They came in from the landward side of the ships, which meant that the target was silhouetted against

D

the afterglow. They dropped down, one by one, and released their bombs. The pilots saw one bomb hit under the stern and they believed they saw another hit amidships. But in the dark, with smoke coming from the anti-aircraft guns and the funnel, they could not be sure.

No Swordfish were lost and no airmen were wounded.

One possible line of attack still open to Admiral Somerville, this late in the day, was attack by submarine. He had sent *Proteus* out to patrol the area north of the force during the day, but at 2150 hours he ordered it to move in towards the Cap de l'Aiguille. *Pandora* was also brought in and both submarines were ordered to attack any French ships they might encounter, *Pandora* was also told that *Strasbourg* might arrive at Algiers sometime after 2300 hours that night.

One more effort might be made in the morning. Admiral Somerville and Admiral Wells decided to get into a position from which *Ark Royal* could launch a strike at dawn. But at 0400 hours, the force ran into thick fog. They waited eagerly for two and a half hours, and then Admiral Wells sadly reported that there was no hope of carrying out the strike in such weather. They would have to abandon the effort.

Admiral Somerville took stock. During the night he had received a message from Admiral Gensoul, saying that his ships were *hors de combat* and he was ordering his naval personnel to evacuate them. So, that much of the operation had been a success. There was no more to be gained by staying at sea; no chance of finding *Strasbourg* now, and considerable danger from German air and submarine attacks. So the admiral set a course for Gibraltar and by 1900 hours Force H was safely 'home'.

With the exception of those ships that had escaped, the operation had been successful enough. Three Swordfish and two Skuas had been lost, but only one Skua crew was missing.

Admiral Somerville was not well satisfied. He had not realized during the day, while he was waiting for Admiral Gensoul to act, that his continual postponements of the strike had prevented *Ark Royal* from having enough planes in the air to spot the escaping *Strasbourg* and launch a strike soon enough to stop her.

In retrospect, Admiral Somerville had some reservations about the entire operation. If only Admiral Gensoul had been willing to see Captain Holland in the beginning, perhaps they could have worked out an arrangement that would have been acceptable to London. The French were, for that matter, not far from meeting the conditions, when they spoke of taking the ships to the Western side of the Atlantic; but just then the knotty question of doing it had not been resolved.

Admiral Gensoul simply did not believe the danger of a German takeover was imminent. The British were certain it was. That was the point of contention.

Admiral Somerville had a hunch that if Holland had only been granted more time, he might have worked out an arrangement acceptable to the French that would have met Britian's demands, but time had run out. The message from the Admiralty had indicated Somerville had delayed long enough if not too long by late afternoon. The issue had to be resolved by nightfall.

The admiral had high praise for all involved, and not the least of them the men of *Hood*, which at that time was not carrying the additional ratings needed for a flagship. But every man had turned to, and two had done the work of three during this operation.

And so Operation Catapult ended. It had not been a very happy one from *Hood*'s point of view, because no one aboard really felt the French were the enemy. However, that was the way of this war, all topsy-turvy so far. What *Hood* needed was a spot of real seagoing action.

10

The Mediterranean

The French affair at Mers-el-Kebir was the most exciting development in the Mediterranean. During the next few days another bombing attack was launched against Mers-el-Kebir to ensure that *Dunkerque* was out of action. While *Bretagne* had sunk and *Provence* had burned, *Dunkerque* had been beached and it was hard to say from a distance how badly damaged she was.

But after 8 July she was definitely out of action, and no ship flying the French flag except *Strasbourg*, which escaped to Toulon, was at large anywhere in the waters of the Mediterranean. In a way, that was a shame. They would have been an invaluable acquisition for the British.

For now, anticipating victory for the Axis powers, Mussolini had decided to enter the war and enjoy its fruits. The Italians wanted more territory in North Africa, and believed it would be cheap to acquire with the preoccupation of the British in the north.

The Italian fleet measured up well against what Britain could spare for the Mediterranean that summer. The British strength was just the regular Mediterranean Fleet and Force H, while the Italians had five capital ships ready for action, one more just finished and many smaller craft. However, they had no thought of engaging the British in an open battle. They said they would depend on the submarine and the bomber. That would finish Britain's naval power in the Mediterranean. In July the Italians started hit and run raids, using cruisers, smaller ships and air power to try to break Britain's strength.

On 8 July, after a few days' rest, Force H was out again, this time heading for Majorca, where *Ark Royal* was to launch an assault against the Italian naval base at Cagliari in southern Sardinia.

On the morning of 9 July all was well and the ships moved pleasantly through the calm sea, the horizon blue and clear of any enemy aircraft. But afternoon came, and with it the first sign of trouble. A big Italian flying boat circled the force and everyone on board *Hood* knew that up there a radio operator was sending signals to the Italian bases. Would it be fleet action, or would it be air attack?

It was an air attack, and it materialized late in the afternoon. The big two-engined Italian bombers came over in formation and very high. Their main target was *Ark Royal*, but enough of them devoted their rain of death to *Hood* to keep everyone on board moving rapidly. The pom-poms and the long-range anti-aircraft guns opened up. The bombs came down, some of them close enough to throw bits of shrapnel against *Hood*.

That attack ended, but another came as the sun sank, and when that was over, yet another attack was made before darkness.

Meanwhile, south of Crete, Admiral Cunningham and the Mediterranean Fleet had encountered an Italian force that was trying to attack two convoys of supply-ships moving from Malta to Alexandria. The Italian force was made up of two battleships, a large number of cruisers and twenty-five destroyers. The fleet gave chase and ran the Italians back into their own waters, where they sought the safety of shore guns. They managed to hit one cruiser and an air attack damaged another.

The Italians responded with more heavy bombing, again from high altitudes, but it was not too effective and no hits were scored. The proposed raid on Cagliari was cancelled. It had been planned with the purpose of diverting the Italians from the big convoys. Now it was not needed.

So it was back to Gibraltar for Force H, and only then did the enemy manage to strike one serious blow. Just outside the entrance to the base a submarine managed to torpedo the destroyer HMS *Escort*. She sank while under tow into port.

The Italians nearly swamped the air-waves during the next few hours, making enormous claims of a victory over the British fleet. The reports said they had either sunk or badly damaged both *Hood* and *Ark Royal*. *Hood* was left on fire and she had been forced to return to England, according to a later report.

Hood and the rest of Force H were out again late in July to mount an attack on Cagliari for certain. On the night of 1 August, planes took off from *Ark Royal* to strike the base. They did so, and then the force returned to Gibraltar. That was all there was to it, easy as falling off a log, or so it seemed.

That brought to an end the Mediterranean cruise. *Hood* was really only on loan to the Mediterranean fleet. She was carried on the lists as part of the Battle-Cruiser Squadron and she was wanted back at Scapa Flow. So she left the warm, Mediterranean sun for the uncertain waters of her native northern shores.

II

'Nothing of Interest to Record'

Late summer 1940 was a difficult time for the Home Fleet. The Nazi u-boats were getting into their stride. Indeed on the trip south in early summer, Force H had been tracked by *U-46*, which actually fired a spread of torpedoes at *Ark Royal* and missed, Neither the admiral nor the men knew that they had been the object of so much concentrated interest.

But in the late summer the u-boat successes had begun to increase and Winston Churchill had begun a frantic search for every type of vessel that could be used in convoy and search work.

One problem of course, was that the fall of France had given Germany a whole new set of bases: Lorient, Brest, La Palice, St Nazaire and La Baule. In late summer u-boats were dispersed to these bases to assemble the wolf-packs that were later to range the North Atlantic so successfully.

In September it became obvious that the Germans were preparing an invasion of England. Barges and tugs jammed the French channel ports. They called it Operation Sealion, and, for a time at least, it was a reality in the minds of the German General Staff. The Battle of Britain had been a struggle for command of the air that summer and it had changed Hitler's plans.

But in the sea, or rather under it, the Germans were proceeding much more efficiently and dangerously. Winston Churchill's most serious concern in the autumn of 1940 was the growing German capacity to sink allied ships and thus cut off England from supplies.

The shortage of escorts was so great that convoys coming to Britain had no protection at all until two or three days before they reached the North Channel. The British secured old destroyers from the US and used every conceivable craft to help fill the gap.

In September and October what was called 'the era of the grey wolves' reached its peak. The U-boats were out in force, and they were proving themselves highly successful. *Hood* had her share of convoy protection duty, but she was essentially flagship of the Battle-Cruiser Squadron, and as such she had the greater duty.

On 16 October *Hood* went out, screened by the destroyers *Somali*, *Eskimo* and *Mashona* to cover *Berwick*, *Norfolk* and *Furious*, while the carrier operated aircraft for an attack on Tromsø. The attack scheduled for the eighteenth was cancelled because of fog, so that the force was broken up. *Hood* went off to Pentland Firth to practice firing her 4-inch guns.

She was in considerable danger on this voyage, because the Germans had managed to mine the area around Hoxa Gate. Three mines were found and swept, but then *Mendip* suffered an explosion of unknown causes and everybody was concerned once again. *Mendip* had at the time been exercising about three miles southeast of the Barrel of Butter. The alert came and all ships were directed not to enter Hoxa until further orders.

Then it was discovered that the explosion in *Mendip* had been due to internal causes: some of her depth-charges had gone off accidentally. The flap was over.

On 25 October, *Hood* had a welcome visitor. The American observer, Lieutenant-Commander Ernest M. Eller left *Norfolk*, which was scheduled for a refit on the Tyne, and went aboard *Hood* to see how America's closest ally operated her big warships under fire. Three days later, the Home Fleet commanded Vice-Admiral Whitworth, commander of the

Battle-Cruiser Squadron, to move out in chase of a possible raider loose somewhere in the north.

Hood sailed, accompanied by *Repulse, Furious, Dido* and *Phoebe*. She was also screened by eight destroyers. The fact was that a German raider was out and she was the pocket battleship *Admiral Scheer*.

Captain Theodor Krancke had taken her to sea on 23 October from Gotenhaven. He had been skilful and lucky, making good use of his radar to avoid unidentified ships, and fortunate enough to move northwards unobserved by British aircraft on patrol. In the north he had been aided by heavy weather, which culminated in a hurricane during the passage through the Denmark Strait. *Admiral Scheer* was uncomfortable in that storm, but she was safer from the British than she could have been at any other time. It was so dreadful in the towering waves that two men were washed overboard and lost. However, for a major German warship, that was a small price to pay for having run the blockade of the Home Fleet and the fearsome Battle-Cruiser Squadron.

In the Reich the *B-Dienst*, the German intelligence service, had been monitoring British wireless communications, and had learned that Convoy HX 84 had left Halifax on 27 October bound for England. Here was a target worthy of *Admiral Scheer*, the first surface vessel of the German Navy to appear in the Atlantic since the death of the *Graf Spee* off Montevideo.

So *Admiral Scheer* was now hunting the convoy. Captain Krancke sent his little observation plane out when the weather permitted and received reports that were at first negative. He had expected little more. He plotted the apparent course of the slow convoy and he knew it would not be long before he found it.

Meanwhile, the Battle Squadron, out searching and finding nothing, was well off the track and soon back at Scapa Flow. On 5 November in the middle of the morning

Captain Krancke again despatched the little Arado aircraft from its catapult. It disappeared off into the southwest sky and Lieutenant Peitsch, the pilot, had specific instructions. If he sighted HX 84 he was to stay out of sight, remain silent, return and report.

Krancke wanted no slip-ups such as British wireless interception that might jeopardize his mission. Nothing happened for several hours. Then at 1430 hours a single steamship came into sight. Krancke was annoyed and disappointed. If he were to attack, the ship might send sos signals. That would certainly warn the convoy. If he were to slip around and try to avoid the ship, he might be spotted, and then he would have neither prize nor surprise.

So Krancke moved swiftly towards the other ship and ordered it to stop and not to use its wireless. The prize was the banana boat *Mopan*, 5,000 tons. Krancke considered putting a prize crew aboard and sending her into a French port, but he was in too big a hurry. According to his calculations, the convoy might appear momentarily over the horizon and so he must dispose of this prize. He took the crew off and began to shell her. At 1605 she sank.

Krancke had been precisely right: the convoy became visible to the naked eye, off in southern waters, just as the banana boat sank.

Admiral Scheer's presence had been successfully concealed for days now. Even the Battle-Cruiser Squadron had not found her. And so when a large modern warship began moving down on the convoy, there was concern but no immediate panic.

From a steamer at the convoy's head came the query, 'What ship?' That was common procedure and did not even denote unusual suspicion. Krancke looked through his glasses. The ship questioning him was an armed merchantman; one of Britain's auxiliary cruisers, no doubt. She would have naval crew aboard and could be expected to react swiftly and without fear. 'Don't answer,' he ordered the signalman on the bridge of *Admiral Scheer*.

The German pocket battleship was closing the range, but the affair with the banana boat had cost them time and speed, and they were still sixteen miles from the convoy. Krancke debated on when to open fire, and decided to wait until he could use both his medium as well as long-range guns. That way he could wreak the maximum havoc in the minimum time; and no one knew how much time he might have.

The ship whose Aldis lamps were blinking so furiously at *Admiral Scheer* was HMS *Jervis Bay*, whose captain, E. S. F. Fegen, was becoming more suspicious every moment of the warship bearing down on him.

The difficulty, of course, was that *Admiral Scheer* was bows-on to the convoy, which made identification almost impossible. She was grey as were British ships and she was not answering *Jervis Bay*'s frantic signals. However, that was often the way with the arrogant, big ships and it hardly seemed cause for alarm.

Admiral Scheer moved on steadily at high speed. *Jervis Bay* continued on course, her Aldis lamps not stopping. Half an hour after sighting the convoy, Captain Krancke decided the range was right. He was ten miles from the convoy when he gave his orders. *Admiral Scheer* wheeled, hove to, turned her broadside to the convoy and unlimbered her 11-inch turrets.

In the moment of turning, of course, the officers aboard *Jervis Bay* knew which ship it was. The profiles of the German pocket battleships were etched on the naval mind. But it was far too late.

Jervis Bay turned towards *Admiral Scheer* and began to advance, while setting off flares to warn the convoy to run for it. Obediently the merchant ships headed south away from the dreaded enemy, while *Jervis Bay* headed directly for him.

It was no contest and no one believed it could be – even a 14,000-ton armed merchantman against a pocket battleship. In less than two hours *Jervis Bay* was aflame and sinking, while the raider turned her attention elsewhere.

The first word that reached the fleet came three hours later; a report that ss *Rangitiki*, a troop convoy in HX 84 was under fire. Then came signals about *Jervis Bay* and from ss *Cornish City*. However, by the time they arrived *Admiral Scheer* was shelling the tanker *San Demetrio*, which began to burn fiercely in the gathering darkness.

Admiral Scheer pressed on searching in the darkness. *Jervis Bay*'s sacrifice had been worthwhile in the sense that she had given the convoy a chance to disperse which made it harder for the raider to find victims.

At 2040 hours that night, following a pre-arranged plan, *Admiral Scheer* stopped firing and 'disappeared'. Captain Krancke had shot off only half his ammunition and he could have kept going. But the German Admiralty's plan for use of the pocket battleships as raiders called for them to hit and run, and so keep the British guessing. In other words they were to destroy some ships, make it into a French port and then wait for another chance and go out and do it again. *Admiral Scheer* headed for the continent.

She would be back, the captain believed, to create maximum disorganization of the British supply and convoy systems just as Admiral Raeder had ordered.

Admiral Scheer had sunk seven ships and damaged three others, so that the Raeder estimate was not far wrong, if the system could be maintained.

When the word came to Scapa Flow that a raider of the *Graf Spee* class was out and had caught HX 84 in the Atlantic, the Home Fleet was widely dispersed. How they were placed gives a fair indication of the situation and troubles of the Fleet at that moment.

Nelson, flagship of the commander of the Home Fleet, was

at Scapa Flow. So was *Rodney*, *Hood*, *Repulse*, *Naiad*, *Bonaventure*, *Dido* (which was unfit for sea), *Phoebe*, *Southampton*, *Cossack*, *Maori*, *Brilliant*, *Electra*, *Somali*, *Mashona*, *Matabele*, *Punjabi*, *Eskimo*, *Keppel*, *Douglas* and *Vimy*.

Australia was on the Clyde and the remaining four ships of the First Cruiser Squadron were either abroad on assignment or being repaired. *Sussex* had suffered bomb damage recently, *Suffolk* had also, and *Norfolk* was undergoing structural repairs.

Of the Second Cruiser Squadron the only effective ship was *Aurora* and she was at Sheerness. *Arethusa* was being repaired for collision damage. *Galatea* had struck a mine and *Penelope* had gone aground.

Of the Tenth Cruiser Squadron, *Nigeria* was at Plymouth, *Kenya* was on the Clyde having not finished with her working-up, and *Fiji* was being repaired for damage suffered by a German torpedo.

Of the Eighteenth Cruiser Squadron, *Manchester* was on the Humber, *Newcastle* was at Plymouth, *Edinburgh* was at Scapa Flow working up after recommissioning, and *Birmingham* was being repaired.

Ten other destroyers were under repair or refit, and seven were operating on the western approaches as escorts and search vessels. *Furious* was about to undergo repairs to her rudder and so she was not available.

The Admiralty thought they had a pretty good idea of what *Admiral Scheer* was up to. In their estimate, the first suggestion was that she was on a 'hit-and-run' raid and would either return to Germany or, more likely, to a port in France, either Brest or Lorient. They could not have been further from the mark.

Hood and the rest of the Battle-Cruiser Squadron, together with reinforcements, set out to cover the approaches to Brest and Lorient. But almost immediately the Admiralty ordered several of the ships to the last known position of

Admiral Scheer to destroy her should she still be there. Of course she was not.

Nelson, *Rodney*, *Southampton* and several other ships moved out to cover the Iceland–Faeroes passage, just in case she should decide to make it back to Germany.

They all missed her and she got clean away.

Hood then returned to Scapa Flow and worked out of there for the rest of November. On 29 November she went to sea again to cover the laying of a minefield northwest of Iceland. If anything could be done to prevent another break-out by a German pocket battleship, it would be. That much was apparent.

12

Attrition

What the Admiralty had not known about *Admiral Scheer* was that she had big fuel tanks, a supply ship '*Nordmark*' out in the Atlantic waiting for her and one of the lowest rates of fuel consumption of any of the large ships. What they had believed to be her *modus operandi* was in fact to be that of *Hipper*, the heavy cruiser which had none of her endurance.

Hipper had escaped as had *Admiral Scheer* through the Denmark Strait in the bad weather of December. On 24 December at 2000 hours, she found a convoy. By this time she was off the coast of Spain, searching for ships on the West Africa–Britain run.

The convoy was protected by several ships, including HMS *Berwick*, which engaged *Hipper*, and a pair of light cruisers, *Bonaventure* and *Dunedin*. In the battle, *Berwick* was hit and then *Hipper* escaped, sinking one 'loner', a British steamer, on her way to the French coast. *Hipper* did, indeed, put in at Brest and she was scheduled to follow the plan the German Admiralty had in mind for *Admiral Scheer*.

The men of *Hood* were vaguely aware of *Hipper*'s shadow during this month. *Hood*, flying still the flag of the Battle-Cruiser Squadron, was at Scapa Flow just before Christmas, carrying out gunnery practice with the Home Fleet. On Christmas Eve she sailed with five other ships to patrol the Iceland–Faeroes passage with the object of intercepting *Hipper*, or any other German ships that might be trying to break out or return to Germany. But after five days at sea she was back, the men having had a cold, wet Christmas. *Hood, Edinburgh*, the destroyers *Cossack, Echo, Electra* and *Escapade* had been north of the Shetlands and east of the Faeroes, where the wind howled down from the Arctic Circle and the fog rolled in reducing visibility to nil.

At New Year's Eve she was at Scapa Flow, the crew could thank the Lord. Before the Christmas sailing, great numbers of turkeys and hams had been ordered up and at last the men had a chance to feast.

However, by 3 January they were back at sea with all the usual little troubles and worries that demanded their attention. That morning off Dunnet Head light, the port paravane fell foul of a mine mooring. The mooring was cut and a destroyer had to be sent to blow up the mine. It was the sort of difficulty that wasted time but had to be taken into account.

On 6 January a youngster joined the great battle-cruiser, a midshipman named W. C. Dundas, and he was soon enveloped inside those decks learning his role in the management of the ship.

It was patrol after patrol. On 12 January at sea in the usual, rotten weather they scoured the patrol zone for enemy craft, but saw only one fishing vessel. *Hood* detached the destroyer *Eskimo* to investigate, but it was just an honest fisherman.

On 17 January *Hood* was in Rosyth, this time to change ammunition and pick up supplies. Such times in port had to be used in a dozen ways that were not possible at sea. One mournful bit of work was a court martial. Out of it one able bodied seaman left the ship under guard, bound for His Majesty's prison at Edinburgh. In time of war, as in time of peace, discipline had to be maintained, and there were men who could not live under authority.

Such work was forgotten as soon as possible, for it was among the least pleasant parts of a sailor's life. The minor refitting finished, *Hood* was back on His Majesty's business again before the end of the month, out in the grey, cold weather of the Atlantic, fighting the snow, the sleet and the fog.

In February she was at Rosyth, getting more of that bits-and-pieces refit that always seemed to be needed these days. What it meant, of course, was a long leave for the starboard watch, and that was much to be desired. But for the others it meant cleaning, painting and provisioning the ship.

On 15 February Captain R. Kerr CBE joined the ship. At 1140 that morning he addressed the ship's company for the first time. Three hours later Captain Glennie left the ship, piped over the side for the last time. The Rev. R. W. Beardmore, the chaplain, also left the ship that day. Finally, the starboard watch returned from their long leave on 26 February.

Patrol in poor weather was almost impossible. A pocket battleship could pass by a mile away and never be seen. Radar, of course, made a difference, but there was still something about being out in the cold, in the fog and in storms that gave one a feeling of futility. One felt one would never come to grips with the enemy, no matter how hard the try.

As for that enemy, the successes of *Admiral Scheer* and *Hipper* had lent credence to Admiral Raeder's plan of using his fast capital ships to harry the British. As the year ended and 1941 began, the German Admiralty decided to increase this type of activity.

Early in February, the battleships *Gneisenau* and *Scharnhorst*, taking advantage of the miserable weather that made the north barely patrollable at all, sailed through the Denmark Strait escaping the British blockade. They sailed up dangerously close to the Arctic pack-ice and then out into open water. For the first time in history German battleships were at large in the Atlantic Ocean. As everyone knew, these two ships had a wide steaming radius.

Their first encounter with the Royal Navy came on 8 February, with the old battleship *Ramillies*, a veteran of the 1914–18 war. The Germans identified her as they closed on Convoy HX 106, but because she had an armament of 15-inch guns they steamed away and left her convoy alone. They were under orders from Admiral Raeder to do just that. They were to play their hit-and-run game, but if strong enemy forces showed up they were to disengage and run so as to be able to fight another day.

The British, however, did not know what they had seen. *Ramillies* had caught sight only of *Scharnhorst* and her captain thought she was a *Hipper*-class cruiser. Since *Hipper* was missing from Brest and *Admiral Scheer* was out in the Atlantic somewhere, it was these two ships the British thought they had sighted.

Soon enough the truth was known. *Hipper* attacked a convoy east of the Azores in the middle of February, a week later *Admiral Scheer* showed up in the Indian Ocean, and that same day *Gneisenau* and *Scharnhorst* moved back into the North Atlantic shipping lanes and sank five ships. It was then learned that no fewer than six armed merchant raiders had escaped through the blockade. Before the end of the month they were all at work.

The First Sea Lord was then in the position of having to react to German action rather than taking the initiative. Sir Dudley Pound found this irritating and dangerous to the extreme.

On 1 March *Hood* was at Rosyth again for a refit. That very day after the captain had made his mess-deck rounds at 1045 hours, the first part of the port watch was given weekend leave. Waterboats came alongside together with the oiler *Britinex*. On 3 March *Hood* moved from the west wall into No. 2 dock. Then it was scrape and paint. In the middle of this activity on 6 March, George VI came to inspect the ship's company.

Paint, paint, paint; for a week they painted the ship until the smell of it was in every seaman's nostrils and the watches could scarcely wait to get off and go ashore for a few pints to wash it away.

It was 18 March before *Hood* left Rosyth, her paintwork clean and her stowage full of provisions. Under the Forth bridge she went, past the first boom, down the swept channel and past the west Inchkeith gate. Then she was out at sea again, streaming her paravanes against mines that might have been dropped by enemy aircraft, or the submarines that might be expected to sneak into these waters.

She was on her way back to Scapa Flow, that grey, barren place where the fleet lay in wait for the Nazi enemy.

On 15 March Admiral Lütjens, with his battleships *Scharnhorst* and *Gneisenau*, found a number of ships steaming independently in the North Atlantic and very quickly sank thirteen tankers and freighters. Another three were captured, prize crews put aboard and sent to German ports.

London was alerted immediately and certain that this time the attacks had been made by *Scharnhorst* and *Gneisenau*. At 1800 hours the ship *Southgate* sent out a distress signal from the same area where the *Athelfoam* had been attacked the previous night. Less than an hour later came a signal from ss *Deneterton*, and two hours later, one from *Chilean Reefer*, all in the same area.

Rodney was in the area, and very close to the Germans. Indeed, when Admiral Lütjens sighted the British battleship, he turned and ran once more, while *Rodney* stopped to pick up some survivors from *Chilean Reefer*. Rodney had been within fifteen miles of one of those German battleships.

On 17 March the Admiralty was in a flap. The raiders might well be in the Newfoundland area and, if so, they might well sight ships from convoy OB 295 which had dispersed and were now proceeding west independently of each other. The *King George V* was sent to protect them.

Next day *Norfolk* sailed from Scapa Flow to Reykjavik to operate in the Denmark Strait, strengthening the patrol which at that moment consisted of two armed merchant cruisers.

Other ships were despatched to other corners and *Hood* was hauled up short. She had been undergoing a refit for nine weeks and on 18 March sailed from Rosyth for Scapa Flow, but the Admiralty ordered her to stay at sea and join *Queen Elizabeth* and *Nelson* on patrol.

They met up on 20 March. That evening came a report that *Scharnhorst* and *Gneisenau* were 46° 50'N, 21° 25'W, steering north at 20 knots. They had been sighted, said the report, by aircraft from *Ark Royal*. So *Nelson*, *Hood*, *Edinburgh* and *Kenya*, with destroyers, began the search.

Luck was with the Germans again and not with Britain's forces. The weather worsened and the aircraft from *Ark Royal* could not operate that night. Next morning it was as bad. It was evening before an aircraft reported spotting the two big ships again. They were out of range, steering east at 20 knots towards St Nazaire. Early on the morning of 23 March they arrived at Brest.

A few days later *Hipper* and *Admiral Scheer*, travelling separately, made it safely through the Denmark Strait again and ran down the Norwegian and Danish coasts until they reached safe waters and put in at Kiel.

The German Admiralty was jubilant. Who ever said that Britannia ruled the waves?

13

Bismarck

As far as Admiral Raeder was concerned, the performance of the battleships and fast cruisers in the Atlantic during the early months of 1941 had proved all the points he had made to Hitler. The new ocean war was a success. Raeder now wanted to maintain the operations and increase their effectiveness by repeating hit-and-run raids as often as possible.

The Battle of the Atlantic had indeed begun. Britain's concern over the big ships and their forays was as great in its way as was Germany's exultation. The threat of attack by enemy ships on the convoys kept most of the Home Fleet tied down; for after the forays of the winter, Whitehall had decided that a battleship or a heavy cruiser should accompany every convoy. Of course, this meant that the forces available to watch the northern passages were depleted and the Germans had an even greater chance of getting through the Denmark Strait.

Then, too, as spring came, there was still another worry to concern the Admiralty in London. Three major warships were either completed or nearly completed that winter in German yards, and that meant it would be so much the worse in late spring and summer. So great was the danger, that heroic measures were called for.

Scharnhorst and *Gneisenau* were in Brest harbour, and that was not a far run from England's shore by air. *Scharnhorst* was in dry dock undergoing some engine repairs, but *Gneisenau* lay in the outer harbour, apparently ready for sea.

The RAF sent over a force of one hundred bombers to

raid Brest on 30 March. It was a failure. Only one bomb hit the deck of *Gneisenau* and it was a dud.

A week later, however, four Beaufort torpedo-planes flew into Brest and one of them, piloted by Flying Officer Kenneth Campbell, took aim at the *Gneisenau* and never wavered. He came in low, through a hail of anti-aircraft fire, and launched his torpedo from 1,600 feet. A moment later the plane crashed, shot down by the flak; but a moment later the stern of *Gneisenau* erupted in smoke and flames as the torpedo hit home.

Gneisenau was then moved into dry dock and there, several nights later, she was hit again in a massive bombing raid. This time she suffered four direct hits.

This double setback was a blow to the German Naval High Command. Just before *Gneisenau* had been put out of action, Admiral Raeder had made plans to extend the hit-and-run war in the North Atlantic. When the next new moon came at the end of the month and the seas would be dark at night, *Bismarck*, the new super-battleship, *Prinz Eugen* and *Gneisenau* were to go to sea for a combined attack on shipping. Once again this force would be under command of Admiral Gunther Lütjens.

But now the reports from Brest were most disconcerting. The first torpedoing had smashed a propeller-shaft and flooded two engine-rooms. The second bombing had done even more damage and it was now estimated that repairs would take about six months.

Admiral Raeder read the reports, but they in no way deterred him from his plan. He was ready now, with Dönitz's help in the undersea division, to destroy Britain's links with the outside world and bring her to her knees. It was unfortunate that both *Scharnhorst* and *Gneisenau* were out of action, but the new cruiser *Prinz Eugen* was not, and *Bismarck* was nearly ready to go.

Bismarck had been built in Hamburg by Blohm and Voss,

quite outside the agreements laid down in any naval treaty. She was listed as 35,000 tons, but actually she was over 50,000 tons and was the strongest ship in the navy. She was fitted out there in the next eighteen months following her 1939 launching. She soon had the four gun turrets, each weighing a thousand tons and her eight 15-inch guns, which were of course more modern than *Hood*'s. The turrets were known as Anton, Bruno, Caesar and Dora, for the Germans subscribed to a different code – *Hood*'s A and B, X and Y were the equivalent.

By the summer of 1940 she was manned and her captain, Ernst Lindemann, came aboard. He put her in commission on 24 August, while *Hood* was off in the Mediterranean. Some 2,000 men would live aboard her.

On 15 September, *Bismarck* left Hamburg and went down the Elbe to the sea by way of the Kaiser Wilhelm Canal. She began her trials in the safe waters of Kiel Bay. From Kiel she headed for the Bay of Danzig to undertake more trials. Each day there was something new: one day the guns would sound, another day the ship would practise man-œuvring at high speed. In various combinations her Arado aircraft would be flown off to make searches and spot for gunnery practice, land and be recovered.

That spring *Bismarck* was joined by *Prinz Eugen*, which had just been completed at the yards in Kiel. She had eight 8-inch guns and a speed of thirty-two knots. They were a pair, indeed the design was so similar that *Prinz Eugen* at 14,000 tons seemed like a small shadow of *Bismarck* which was three times as large.

The plans were proceeding without break when on 24 April a magnetic mine exploded close to *Prinz Eugen* causing minor damage. It was severe enough to delay any operations until the end of May.

Admiral Raeder now called Admiral Lütjens to Berlin to discuss the question of delay. The operational commander wanted to delay until either *Scharnhorst* was ready to sail or *Tirpitz* was worked up. But Raeder was not really looking for advice. He had his mind made up and so the subordinate had to swallow his own misgivings about the chances of taking on the Home Fleet with so few ships, modern and powerful as they might be.

At the beginning of May, Lütjens travelled to Gdynia to join *Bismarck*.

Hood, with four destroyers, was in Hvalfjord, in accordance with the Admiralty's instructions to the Fleet to keep capital ships available for coverage of convoys. Admiral Tovey in London was much concerned about *Bismarck* and *Prinz Eugen*, expecting a raid at any time. *Hood*'s captain was now R. Kerr, who had taken over from Captain I. G. Glennie. Vice-Admiral Whitworth was still flying his flag in *Hood*, but he would soon be relieved by Vice-Admiral L. E. Holland CBE.

Whitworth had hoisted his flag in *Hood* in the spring of 1939 and he was going to be sorry to leave her. So *Hood* headed back to England, to accomplish the change.

While all this was being accomplished on *Hood*, in Gdynia there was a buzz of activity. On 5 May Adolf Hitler and his staff travelled by a special train to see *Bismarck*. Admiral Lütjens busied himself with his new operational plans, code-named *Rheinabung*, or Rhine Exercise, which were to begin 18 May.

Hitler arrived in a flurry, boarded the yacht *Hela* in the harbour and moved out to where *Bismarck* was lying. He was piped over the side while Admiral Lütjens, Captain Lindemann and 2,000 men waited to receive him. He inspected the ship, paying so much attention to the gunnery operation that he spent nearly a half an hour there. During the visit, Captain Topp of *Tirpitz* came up and begged the Führer to let him go to sea with *Bismarck* on the new operation, but he was refused permission.

The plans continued and the ship took on food and ammunition. There were armour-piercing shells for the eight 15-inch guns; explosive shells for the twelve 5·9-inch guns, and tracer and high explosive for the sixteen 4·1-inch anti-aircraft guns and sixty quick-firing light guns which were good for shooting at planes coming in low.

In other words, she was equal in every way to *Hood* in fighting capacity, much newer and more heavily armoured. After all, *Hood* had been built as a cruiser-killer and had been planned in another war, when naval strategy was very different. She was still a battle-cruiser, not a battleship, although her lines, her reputation and her glory made people in England forget that fact. Indeed, before the war began there had been a cryptic note in her dossier: to be scrapped in 1941. But it was now 1941 and rather than being scrapped, *Hood* was one of the major bastions of Britain's sea defences, all the more so now that the struggle in the Mediterranean completely tied down Admiral Cunningham's Mediterranean Fleet, and the attrition there would be dreadful.

Hood had received some improvements during the last few months. She had a new sort of gunnery radar, nothing quite as elaborate as the firing system that Captain Lindemann had at his disposal, but nevertheless an improvement over the optical range-finders she had used for so long.

Hood's basic problem, however, was that there had been no time since her refit in the spring to have a proper workup. The crew was new and green, and the demands on the Home Fleet that spring had been so great that there simply had been no time to put the ship in order. The men were having to learn on the job.

Operation Rheinabung was considered of major importance by the Germans and now their plans were complete. On 16 May support ships set sail from French and Norwegian ports. Support ships were absolutely essential these days to a German surface-ship operation. *Scharnhorst* and *Gneisenau*'s successes in the Atlantic and elsewhere had been gained only because they were able to refuel and re-supply while at sea. Unlike British ships, they were not built for long periods at sea. German sailors in port did not live on their battleships and their cruisers, but in barracks or on support ships. The facilities were cramped compared with those on British lower decks. German ships were fighting machines, not destined to go around the world but to dart out, fight and dart back into safety so as to be able to fight again. All this meant that *Bismarck* was much more efficient as a fighting machine than *Hood*.

The emphasis of Operation Rheinabung had changed slightly with *Gneisenau* and *Scharnhorst* out of action. Admiral Lütjens had been granted permission for *Bismarck* to put up a fight against a British battleship, if any encounter came to that. But his main purpose was to tie up the big British ships that were now on the convoy routes, thus allowing the lighter German vessels to wreak havoc among the merchantmen.

The enthusiasm of Hitler and the naval staff for the fight that Lütjens wanted evaporated with the knowledge that the *Bismarck* would be out there pretty much alone. In fact, Raeder was so concerned about Hitler's timidity – well known in naval matters – that he did not even tell the Führer when the ships were to sail until after the event.

It was expected now that these two ships would go out for as long as three months, so that eight tankers and support ships were sent out ahead, some to the area south of Greenland and others to the Azores. Four weather ships were sent out to provide constant reports on the weather in various climes, and another tanker was ordered to stand by in Norway.

On the morning of 18 May, all was ready.

14

'The Bismarck is out...'

On *Hood* even in wartime, if the ship was in port, Sunday was an easier day than others. It was a different day and some used the ship's chapel to reinvigorate their spirits. Seamanship and duty done, there was always a bit more relaxation, a better meal and a general feeling of comradeship that transcended that of other days.

But across the Channel, and over inside German waters, there was not the slightest relaxation this May morning, Sunday or no. Admiral Lütjens that morning was holding a meeting of his staff. Captain Lindemann and Brinkmann of *Bismarck* and *Prinz Eugen* were there. The admiral was changing the plan.

They had been scheduled to sail for Korsfjord on the Norwegian coast, and there lie up for a day while *Prinz Eugen* refuelled. Then they were to head for the Atlantic through the gap between Iceland and the Faeroes that German warships had used so successfully during the winter months.

Lütjens was dissatisfied with the plan. He wanted to get out quickly and to do so, he proposed to sail directly to the Arctic without stopping in Norway where British aircraft might very well begin tracking them; to fuel near Jan Mayen island where they would be safe from attack; and speed into the Atlantic through the Denmark Strait before the British could know what was happening. This was the way he had got out with *Scharnhorst* and *Gneisenau*, and even if the Faeroes route was shorter he still preferred the route he knew and had navigated successfully.

By noon these changes had been made and the officers informed. The routine of last minute supply and oiling went on. A few crew changes were taking place in the afternoon. Lütjens went to inspect *Prinz Eugen* and her crew before she sailed later that afternoon of 18 May. It was hardly a secret sailing, for she had been surrounded by reporters and cameramen during the last few hours. The change in crews – including the taking on of a number of men to man the prizes that Lütjens hoped to get – meant that many a bar in the crooked streets off the port would be buzzing that night with tales of the big ships and their mission.

As *Bismarck* weighed anchor and sailed into the Baltic, her band assembled on the quarter deck and played the sentimental song the Germans loved so well, '*Muss i' denn*'. That night the warships moved alone. They were to stay apart from each other to avoid being spotted by the British until they made Arkona, the cape off the Prussian coast, where they would be met by a small fleet of escorts, destroyers and minesweepers.

At Arkona Admiral Lütjens felt it was time to address the men. He spoke briefly of the glories of the navy and the ship, and he told them that they were going on a three-month cruise to destroy British shipping and cripple the enemy lifeline from the west. 'I give you the hunter's toast,' he said in finishing, 'good hunting and a good bag.'

And then they were off, into the grey Baltic, heading north and west. They passed through the Great Belt, which divides Denmark, and the sea was calm. Dawn broke at about the time the admiral was digesting a message which reported that it had not been possible to scout the British fleet anchorage at Scapa Flow on Sunday, as the weather had not permitted. No one knew, therefore, where the major units of the Home Fleet might be.

It was just another little worry on Admiral Lütjens' shoulders. If he had known that *Hood* and *Prince of Wales* were there, he would have felt much better about it. In the morning light, the sea before them was empty, because the German Admiralty had warned away all shipping; no chances of a slip-up were being taken.

But one ship came along, the Swedish cruiser *Gotland*, and she steamed a parallel course along the Swedish coast for several hours, through the Kattegat and the Skagerrak before turning away. She sent a message which so convinced Admiral Lütjens that his presence had been betrayed to the enemy that he informed his headquarters.

Various reports were being spread that night. When *Bismarck* had left Gdynia, an ordinary dockworker had strolled away from the harbour and sent a message that would travel half-way around Europe, via Switzerland and Portugal, before it came to rest on an inconspicuous desk in London. In Kristiansund an agent of the Norwegian resistance saw the bow waves of the German ships as they sped by, and another message was soon on its way to London. From Stockholm came a message to the Admiralty saying much the same. Two large warships, escorted by many destroyers and other vessels and accompanied by aircraft circling overhead, were moving fast to the north.

In a matter of hours, the word came to Admiral Sir John Tovey, commander of the Home Fleet, who was in his flagship the new *King George V*. On the morning of 26 May, the first warning came from London by telephone. Everyone was pretty sure the ships involved were *Bismarck* and *Prinz Eugen*, because London had been following the progress of their work-ups.

There had been enough activity in the North Sea for the admiral to have sensed that something was up. The Germans had increased their reconnaissance of Scapa Flow to several flights a day. Why were they so infernally curious as to which ships were in harbour and precisely when? The attention was not only unwelcome but it was also revealing. And so the news came as no surprise.

That morning Admiral Tovey ordered the cruiser *Suffolk* to keep a sharp eye on her patrol area in the Denmark Strait. He also sent her sister ship *Norfolk* to relieve her, so that she might return for fuelling. The Home Fleet was put on notice to steam.

Even as these messages were sent, the Admiralty had planes flying on searches over the Norwegian fjords. Aboard *Hood*, Captain Kerr had received the message. *Hood* was swift in making ready. Captain Kerr had been in command since February and both officers and ratings were responsive to his ways.

The order also went to *Prince of Wales*, Britain's newest battleship. Sister ship to *King George V*, she was so new that she had not even been properly worked up. However, that was the way of the war this spring. The pressure was on and there was no time for a proper work-up.

On the lower decks and in the engine rooms, no one knew what occasioned the excitement, but they were used to that. Back to Hvalfjord more than likely, was the word that passed along the decks; but some guessed there was more to it this time. They might be getting into a real fight at last.

On the bridge there was an inkling that something very definitely was up. The admiral spoke several times on the special green telephone to London, and that was most unusual.

All these conversations were about preparations to go after two ships which were moving northwards in Norwegian waters.

The cruisers *Manchester* and *Birmingham* together with several trawlers were sent to the Faeroes. So much for the contention of some in Kiel that the Faeroes route would be easier than the other.

As to the fighting units, Admiral Tovey would take *King George V* and the old battle-cruiser *Repulse* in his unit, and Vice-Admiral Holland, commander of the Battle-Cruiser Squadron, would stay in *Hood* and lead *Prince of Wales* out to search for the enemy.

The reconnaissance planes were out that day before noon, and at Scapa Flow, Admiral Tovey waited for the ships to get up steam.

Flying a Spitfire equipped with a camera, Flying Officer Suckling of the RAF headed for the fjords around Bergen. South of Bergen over Grimstad Fjord, he thought he saw something below. He circled, looked at his wristwatch, photographed what he saw and headed back for England. A moment after landing his camera was on its way to the laboratory, while he reported that he had seen two cruisers.

1515 that afternoon, the developed films were in the hands of those who realized that the two ships were not cruisers but *Bismarck* and *Prinz Eugen*.

And so it was official. *Bismarck* was out. The Admiralty had the news at 1545 hours. RAF bomber command could have planes out to attack them before dark. Or could they?

The reports from the weather people indicated otherwise. From the Orkneys came word that the weather was deteriorating, and that by evening operations would be out of the question.

Admiral Lütjens was lucky then. He had not been so lucky earlier that day, for the sighting by the RAF was more than he had bargained for, even though he had known the night before that London knew of his presence. A signal from German Group North had informed him of a British instruction to all coastal aircraft to look out for the German squadron.

It was because of this that Lütjens changed his tactics. He had originally planned to run north and to refuel in the Arctic. Having been discovered, however, he felt it all important not to stop once he left German-controlled waters. So that morning, he had pulled into Grimstad fjord to refuel *Prinz Eugen*, only to be discovered by the RAF Spitfire.

At Scapa Flow the evening brought mist and rain. It threatened to be just the kind of night made for a blockade runner, and Admiral Tovey knew that the Germans would be just as aware of this as he was.

Indeed, in Grimstad fjord, Admiral Lütjens had his weather reports and he was ready. All afternoon, the crews of the two ships had painted. Their object was to wipe out the camouflage markings with which they had come into the area, and leave it in battleship grey, which would indicate that they were British ships.

So as the drizzle settled in over Scapa Flow and Admiral Tovey waited, *Bismarck* weighed anchor and turned north. Soon, she and *Prinz Eugen* were moving together, accompanied by three destroyers. When they reached the open sea they began to zigzag and to move faster. Shortly before midnight they turned due north and began to run for the Arctic Ocean.

Tovey pondered the possible routes that his enemies might take. He waited for news from Bomber Command who were sending planes over Norway. But the planes when they reached the coast saw no ships. The weather was so foul that they could not even say they were not there. The aerial mission had been less than a success.

About two hours after Admiral Lütjens sailed from the Bergen fjords, Admiral Tovey made up his mind. He could not leave these vast stretches of water undefended when he did not know where his enemy was. He instructed *Hood*, with six destroyers, to head for Iceland and to refuel. They were to move southwest of Iceland and cover both the Iceland–Greenland route and the Iceland–Faeroes route.

They moved out in the wet once more towards Hvalfjord. Not a man on board *Hood* knew that he was seeing Scapa Flow for the last time.

15

The Grey, Grey Sea

They steamed along the grey, grey sea. The ships of the opposing navies were not very close at this point, but they were heading for a common destination, Iceland.

At 0500 hours, the German admiral dismissed his destroyers. He was getting so far ahead of them that they would never be able to accompany him on the desperate *durchbrach* out of waters the arrogant British called their own.

At Scapa Flow Admiral Tovey waited. He must have news from Norway before he could do more. And what was the news from Norway? The cloud banks hung low over water and the land, and the sort of news he wanted was not to be had. The patrol planes could see nothing at all. By the middle of the morning it was even worse because all flights were cancelled until further notice. The soup was too thick up there.

One plane did get away that afternoon, however. It was an old American twin-engined Maryland bomber used by a squadron of Albacore torpedo-planes as a target tower. It was rather like a twin-tub washing machine, but it flew.

The Maryland did not get off the ground until 1630 hours and then it flew through cloud so thick that the crew hardly knew when they were almost down at sea-level. The navigator of the aircraft, however, had plotted a steady course and they came down at their estimated time of arrival with the route to Grimstad Fjord right ahead of them. They flew up the fjords and found them empty. They moved around the area, checking Bergen harbour and other waterways, and found nothing, nothing at all of what they had wanted to see. The big grey birds had flown.

Maryland returned to the airfield at Hatston, across the way from Scapa Flow, and before it landed had sent its message to all who had been waiting for it. There were no enemy warships in any of the fjords around Bergen.

So at last Admiral Tovey knew. Now he could act, and he began getting the message away. The aircraft-carrier *Victorious* would come along even though her aircrews were green; so too would the cruisers *Galatea*, *Hermione*, *Kenya*, *Aurora* and half a dozen destroyers. He sent a message to *Repulse*, which was on her way to join him north of the Hebrides in the morning. He was then ready to move. At 2015 hours he sailed.

Suffolk had already been despatched to join *Norfolk* in the Denmark Strait, and *Arethusa* had been sent to join *Birmingham* and *Manchester* in the Iceland–Faeroes passage.

Where would the Germans go? Actually on the morning of 22 May Admiral Lütjens was still not quite firmly decided whether he ought to move north or south of Iceland once he had rounded the northern tip of his enemy's territory. The indecision caused Admiral Dönitz and the submarine fleet to be prepared for either course. But finally Lütjens decided to stick to his original plan. He would head directly for the Denmark Strait in the foul weather that persisted.

Intelligence was the most difficult commodity to come by this day. Admiral Lütjens fretted in the *Bismarck*, because he had no idea where his enemies were. The Luftwaffe's reconnaissance of Scapa Flow had been cut off by the same weather that so hampered the British pilots trying to trace the Germans in Norway. For once, too, the monitoring of British naval traffic did not the slightest bit of good to

B-*dienst*. There was no indication of any activity by the Home Fleet that was out of the ordinary.

At noon the squadron altered course and the men were put to work painting out the Nazi swastikas on the quarter-decks and forecastles. *Bismarck* and *Prinz Eugen* were out of German aircraft range now and the swastikas had done nothing but obviate whatever good might have been done by changing the colour of the ships.

In the weather they were passing through the effort hardly seemed necessary. The fog was so thick that afternoon that at times *Bismarck* could not see *Prinz Eugen* at all, and had to shine a searchlight aft so that the cruiser was able to follow in her wake. If they had wanted bad weather for a break-out they certainly had it.

Admiral Lütjens also had some comforting news from the Luftwaffe that afternoon. Reconnaissance planes had flown over Scapa Flow during a break in the weather and had sighted three big ships, a carrier and many cruisers and destroyers. The implication was that no ships had sailed out of Scapa Flow since the last reconnaissance flights. This was a visual report, not photographic, because the cloud cover had been such that the photographs did not come out.

The fact was, therefore, that *Hood* and *Prince of Wales* had irrevocably sailed, and Admiral Lütjens had no idea of it.

By the middle of that night *Bismarck* and *Prinz Eugen* were 200 miles northeast of Iceland and this was the crucial moment. Lütjens did not waver, he ordered the ships to turn southwest for the run through the Denmark Strait.

The meteorologists aboard *Bismarck* were urging speed if the squadron was going to make the run, because, they said, they had indications that the weather would soon clear, and that was precisely what Admiral Lütjens did not want. They upped the speed to 27 knots. In an hour, however, they had to slow to 24 knots, because they were travelling through mushy ice. It was hard going and it made the officers nervous, but there was no recourse. They were committed.

As dawn came up, the weather continued foggy and cloudy, the sea calm. They moved through it and through the ice.

By the middle of the morning they were about to reach the narrow passage, only about forty miles wide, which separated the Greenland icefloes from the limits of the minefield the British had laid north from Iceland. They saw the pack.

Back they went to 27 knots for this crucial passage. If they could get through unobserved, they would be out in the Atlantic and all the plans made in Berlin could be carried out.

But in the late afternoon just as they were in the middle of the run, the weather began to clear. They could see the white-capped mountains of Greenland off to starboard, and ice, miles and miles of it stretching out like a greenish plain.

On the bridges of the two ships, the look-outs and the officers maintained their watch. They could see little to port, for here the fog rose up out of Iceland and came towards them with no indication of what was behind it. In fact the British cruisers were behind it and not very far away.

Aboard *Suffolk* Captain Robert Ellis had been searching. His ship had been in the Straits so many times in recent days that it seemed almost their destiny to be there. On the eighteenth he had responded to Admiral Tovey's order to take on fuel by heading swiftly back to Hvalfjord on the west shore of Iceland, and had then returned to the Strait once again.

Meanwhile, *Norfolk*, flying the flag of Admiral Frederick Wake-Walker of the First Cruiser Squadron, had steamed to Isafjördhur, on Iceland's northwestern peninsula, where

Suffolk was to join her so that they could patrol together.

At 1000 hours on 23 May, therefore, as Admiral Lütjens was moving into the narrow passage, the British were indeed not far away.

Suffolk came into the entrance to Isafjördhur, and *Norfolk*'s Aldis lamp began to blink. The instructions were passed: *Suffolk* was to proceed up to the pack-ice opposite Vesfirdir, and to patrol parallel to it. This could be done by radar. *Norfolk* would be some fifteen miles south of her, in case the Germans preferred to risk the edge of the minefield rather than the northern waters. The two cruisers would meet next morning to compare notes.

So Captain Ellis turned *Suffolk* and made for the edge of the pack, where he found clear water along the edge, and as good a view of Greenland's mountains as Admiral Lütjens was enjoying. He was to patrol a line running southwest–northeast, travel to a designated point, about three hours steaming in all, and then reverse his course.

On the leg running northeast, *Suffolk* could stay in the open water near the ice, for with her radar she could detect the coming of the German squadron before she could be seen. On the return leg the radar – still in its infancy – was blind. Therefore Ellis steered along the edge of the fog bank so that he could slip into it if the Germans should appear. It was not *Suffolk*'s task to get blown to bits, which would have been an easy enough matter for *Bismarck*'s 15-inch guns. The cruiser was to be the eyes of the fleet and was to shadow the Germans once they were sighted.

The afternoon of 23 May passed slowly, the sea swelling gently as the British cruiser patrolled back and forth along the edge of the pack-ice.

Meanwhile, coming up from the south, *Hood* and her force were doing much the same, patrolling, watching, looking for hour upon hour for the enemy.

Bismarck and *Prinz Eugen* moved along in the failing daylight, heading out to complete their breakthrough into the Atlantic where they would play hob with the British. There were convoys out there which Admiral Lütjens wanted to hunt.

Suffolk was moving southwest on her apparently endless patrol, when at 1800 hours the look-outs were changed. Able Seaman Newell took over as starboard-after-look-out on the heated bridge of the cruiser. In heavy weather it was not easy to keep awake; the combination of the lulling motion and the warmth almost sent one to sleep.

Newell picked up his binoculars and started to watch his sector. He would sweep up to a given point, stop for a moment and move the glasses back; again, and again and again. An hour went by and he saw nothing.

The minutes dragged, five more, ten and then fifteen. He was sweeping, swee . . . And he stopped. The glasses moved back, and he started. For there, framed in the lenses was a great black shape, an immense warship slipping out of the mist not seven miles away.

Able Seaman Newell immediately sang out, 'Ship bearing Green One Four O.' He continued to look and another ship, smaller, but of the same general appearance came into view behind the other. 'Two ships . . .'

Captain Ellis heard and before looking he saw to the safety of his own ship. He ordered the helmsman to turn hard to port and seek the safety of the yellow fog bank.

One of his officers pressed the alarm bell and the crew of *Suffolk* sprang to action stations as the course was altered. The manœuvre was so swift that in the wardroom crockery went crashing to the deck.

Captain Ellis gave another order. 'Signal to Admiralty,' he said quickly. 'Most immediate: *Bismarck* and cruiser in sight. . . .' They were heading south as Ellis reported their position.

Suffolk seemed to inch into the fog. Those on the bridge felt a prickling sensation on the back of their necks as they waited for the screaming, the booming and the possible flashes that would mean *Bismarck* had unlimbered her 15-inch guns. A minute went by and some held their breaths.

Another minute went by and then the tendrils of the fog, the wonderful, enveloping, hiding fog began to cover them. *Suffolk* disappeared inside the blanket, only her wake betraying her for a moment or two.

Just before they moved inside they saw *Bismarck* clearly, her bow wave high as she travelled at high speed past them. Then they were on radar and they watched the blips move along, inching ahead in what was in reality a movement of miles.

The signals went below to coding and then to the wireless operators. Within a few minutes they were supposed to be received in the War Room of the Admiralty. More messages went out, this time to Admiral Tovey and the other searchers. *Bismarck* had been found, and the chase was on.

Once *Bismarck* had run safely by and was at the limit of *Suffolk's* radar range, Captain Ellis came out of the sheltering fog and began to shadow her. She followed from a distance of about thirteen miles behind *Prinz Eugen*, just at the outside edge of the radar range.

Norfolk received the news while she was deep inside the fog-belt, so that Captain Alfred Phillips steered for the open water to the north. He was unlucky. He emerged from the fog just six miles from *Bismarck*, and she was coming straight at him.

Admiral Lütjens wasted no time. The moment the shape was identified as a ship, the guns were aimed and within moments were firing. Captain Phillips turned and ran for the safety of the fog, but before he could get there *Bismarck* had fired five salvoes. The first came within 50 yards of the bridge and one shell struck the water and actually ricocheted over the ship. The other shots were nearly as close and fountains of water 150 feet high rose above her.

This was good shooting by anybody's standards. The modern range-finders and training mechanisms of the Germans were not to be underestimated. Splinters fell on board *Norfolk* and she suffered some heavy hits to her plating, but neither ship nor anyone in the crew was hurt. Moments later the glorious fog closed in around them and they were safe.

For the moment, however, the British reaction was delayed. *Suffolk*'s wireless messages had not got through to the Admiralty, because her aerials had iced up and the signals had not carried much past *Norfolk*. It was not until considerably later that signals from *Norfolk* warned all at sea that *Bismarck* had been found.

16

The Chase

When the wireless room in *Hood* received the first sighting report from *Norfolk*, she, *Prince of Wales* and their destroyers were just 300 miles away from *Bismarck* and *Prinz Eugen* and were steering a course that would converge with that of the German squadron in half a day or less. They could expect to be in contact some time after 0200 hours.

Admiral Holland was not eager for a night engagement, and he demanded a course that would intercept his enemies an hour before sunrise. One was worked out and the information passed to *Prince of Wales*. A little later Captain Kerr told the men of the ship what was happening.

Here it was at last. All those weeks and months of poking about the North Sea and the North Atlantic without a taste of real action were about to be forgotten. *Bismarck* was out, *Suffolk* was shadowing her and *Hood* and *Prince of Wales* were going to intercept. The ship would go to action stations shortly after midnight, and so every man off watch was to get all the rest he could. The same message was sent across to *Prince of Wales*.

So now the two great British ships, moving at 27 knots, sped through the heavy seas, forecastles and bridges at times hidden completely by sea and spray. The weather was deteriorating again, badly. Visibility was very poor, fog and rain were beginning to give way to snow squalls, and the sea was acting up so much that the destroyers could not keep up and had to drop astern.

It was 2000 hours when these first reports came in and

the ships moved to flank speed. Admiral Holland was hurrying into action and he wondered how ready *Prince of Wales* was for it. She had not really been tried yet; in fact a number of civilian workmen were still on board. Having come along to Scapa Flow to work her up, check the guns and all the rest, they had found themselves trapped on board when the Admiralty ordered the ship to sail in pursuit of *Bismarck*.

On this long chase Admiral Holland had given his gunners as much practice as possible and had laid down a few orders. If the ships were together when they met the enemy, they would concentrate their fire. If they were not, they would fire independently.

So the ships sped on through the night. The gunnery officers on board both ships fussed and fiddled, and made calculations to suit themselves.

On board *Prince of Wales* the civilian engineers and workmen moved about in the engine room and the turrets. The 14-inch guns had not been quite reliable and they would soon have their work cut out for them.

On board *Hood* there was no such lack of confidence in the weapons. She had been built to be a fighting platform with those four huge turrets and the eight 15-inch guns, each of which fired a shell that weighed nearly a ton. It took a team of men to work those guns, but they had practised plenty of times and were a fighting team.

Hood had radar but it was only an adjunct to her fighting strength. Each turret had its own range-finder and the observations were fed into a central transmitting station which worked out the mathematics and passed the figures on to the gunnery officer. It was all there in a jiffy; *Hood*'s own course and speed, the course and speed of the enemy and her bearing in relation to *Hood*.

Hood's turrets revolved completely. They were first designed in World War I and had been modified after

Jutland proved how vulnerable turrets such as these were.

In fact, Admiral Horace Hood was killed at Jutland when his flagship *Invincible* blew up, and it was partly because of this that *Hood*'s turrets had been modified. Under the old system a flash inside a turret could jump from one cordite charge to another all the way down to the ship's magazines. The modification consisted of placing flash-proof scuttles between the magazine and the trunk, so that when handlers were moving ammunition up the trunk they were sealed off from the gun-house above.

That change did not solve a major problem: the lack of armour on the top of the turrets. However, there was not too much that could be done about that. Additional armour would have been a major change that would most certainly have affected the ship's metacentrics, and it might have made her dangerously top-heavy.

Hood's guns had been built and rebuilt time and time again not because there was anything wrong with them, but because they wore out rapidly in action. After 300 firings the rifling was finished and had to be renewed; that is why the big ships needed constantly refitting.

In addition to the big guns *Hood* still had her 5·5-inch guns which were good for low-angle firing against surface targets. The refit she was supposed to have had in 1939 would have involved stripping off these relics and giving her modern guns, but the war had cancelled these plans, and she had to make do with the weapons she already had. Other planned changes that would also have been helpful included an aircraft hangar and alterations to her armour to give better protection horizontally.

It could all have been done. The engineers had figured out that by removing her conning tower, more weight could have been added to her topside without endangering her stability. With the 12-inch armour-belt along most of her sides she was well protected against mines, torpedoes and naval gunfire. But all this had been done before air-craft became an important aspect of naval warfare, and those who knew her best realized that she was woefully vulnerable to attack from above.

She had been given new twin 4-inch anti-aircraft guns and some other protection but it was no solution to the big problem. Luckily, although she had been bombed a number of times in the Mediterranean and in the north, not one had really connected with her and so the armour had not been tested.

On board the *Hood*, however, a man quickly enough for-got about her deficiencies and looked to her strengths. With her graceful lines she was one of the most impressive fighting ships in the world, and most of England still believed that she was the most effective.

So when *Hood* and *Prince of Wales* turned towards the point at which Admiral Holland hoped to intersect the enemy, the crew of the ship were confident that they could handle anything the enemy wanted to inflict on them.

Early in the evening it became apparent that the destroyers would not be able to keep up with the two larger warships. Admiral Holland signalled them just before 2100 hours. 'If you are unable to maintain this speed I will have to go on without you. You should follow at your best speed.'

Leaving the little ships behind, therefore, *Hood* and *Prince of Wales* sped on. *Hood* showed just how wet she could really be in a sea-way as a result of the many helter-skelter modifications that had been made to her over the years.

The destroyers came on rather than be left behind, and the hours flew by. It was late May, the middle of the Arctic spring, and the twilight lasted long before the sun dis-appeared just below the horizon.

Hood was making speed. She was heading towards the encounter. Every man, from the admiral to the lowest rank and the greenest boy, was ready, waiting and confident.

17

Bismarck's *Run*

Aboard *Bismarck*, Admiral Lütjens knew the battle had begun in that brief moment when *Norfolk* came rearing blindly out of the fog, saw him, turned and ran back into it before his gunners could get a fair go at her. The blast from the guns had knocked out *Bismarck*'s primitive, forward radar and from that point it was blind. As soon as Admiral Lütjens learned this worrying news, he ordered *Prinz Eugen* to move ahead of *Bismarck* and lead the way. She would be his eyes.

In passing *Prinz Eugen* came close abeam, and as this happened *Bismarck*'s wheel jammed and she began to heel to starboard. Captain Brinkmann on *Prinz Eugen* saw that something was amiss and ordered his ship to steer hard to starboard also. A collision was narrowly avoided.

It was a rapid run, the German ships were moving at nearly 30 knots and *Suffolk* behind them had a hard time keeping up. She vibrated like a victim of St Vitus's dance, but she kept moving.

Admiral Lütjens was still operating under the misapprehension engendered in him by the Luftwaffe's careless observation of Scapa Flow the day before. He did not know that *Hood*, *Prince of Wales* and *King George V* had sailed; he had not the slightest hint that *Repulse*, an aircraft-carrier and any number of lesser ships were all converging on his projected course, bent on blowing him out of the water.

He did know that *Suffolk* behind him was sending out messages throughout the night at fifteen-minute intervals.

Some matelots and even some junior officers wondered why *Bismarck*, pride of the Führer's fleet, was running from a paltry British cruiser. The fact was that Admiral Lütjens was under strict orders to avoid open combat with British ships of war, unless in doing his duty, which was to harry the merchant fleet, he had to fight. However, Lütjens knew that very soon he was going to have to face an attack of some kind.

Wouldn't it come from the air? Did the British have a carrier out somewhere in the North Atlantic that he did not know about? Would it be a submarine attack? That seemed most unlikely given the speed at which *Bismarck* and *Prinz Eugen* were travelling.

The clues began to come in, mostly from the wireless. The operators reported that the British Admiralty had been sending messages throughout the night, some of them clearly addressed to ships other than *Suffolk*. Lütjens, of course, did not know which ships, but on the other hand it was too much to expect that if *Suffolk* was following them, other warships, capital ships, had not also been despatched. But from where and when? Those all important questions hung heavy in the air.

The chase continued. Admiral Lütjens and the German Admiralty – which was decoding the British naval transmissions – soon became aware that no matter what changes in course or speed *Bismarck* and *Prinz Eugen* made, the shadowing *Suffolk* was on to them. Hours later the admiral suddenly realized that the British must have a radar system far superior to the German one. The thought was disquieting.

On *Bismarck* the captain had ordered his men to remain at action stations and they stayed there throughout the long night. On *Prinz Eugen* Captain Brinkmann went to second condition, which meant the men had four hours on watch and four off.

The chase continued. At 2200 hours *Bismarck* suddenly disappeared into a rain storm, and *Suffolk* was afraid that she had lost her. They were almost through the strait and the body of water was widening rapidly. If *Bismarck* could make the last bit of it, get through and out into the Atlantic. . . .

The distance between the British force led by Admiral Holland and the German squadron closed steadily. At one point Admiral Tovey considered sending Holland a message ordering *Prince of Wales*, because she was more heavily armoured, to put ahead so as to draw *Bismarck*'s fire. However he decided against it. It would have been unwarranted interference in the command of a capable officer. So *Hood* steamed on with *Prince of Wales* following.

By 2100 hours the British squadron was travelling at 27 knots. Every man aboard knew where they were going and what they had to do. An hour later the ships began to prepare for battle. In *Hood* the officers were briefed in the wardroom before it was turned into a casualty station. In the cinema on *Prince of Wales* the men queued for the white gloves and hoods that formed their anti-flash gear. In both ships officers and men changed into clean underwear and socks to prevent wounds from infection. As the ships heaved and plunged through the perilous sea, many a letter was written and many a picture brought out in these late hours of the night.

The wise ones took down the photographs of their loved ones and together with anything breakable, wrapped and stowed them away because the pounding of the big guns would almost certainly break them.

Officers and men donned lifejackets. At midnight the admiral ordered them to action stations. Late in the middle watch they considered catapulting the aircraft to have 'eyes', but the weather was much too bad to do this.

The battle ensigns had been hoisted just after the admiral's call to prepare for action. They flapped and snapped in the wind, showing whitely against the dark of night.

At midnight *Suffolk* lost contact with *Bismarck* and did not regain it for nearly two hours. Admiral Tovey was distressed. Where could *Bismarck* have gone?

If the enemy continued on the course and at the speed noted in Suffolk's last despatches, Admiral Holland was about a hundred miles away from *Bismarck* and would cross about sixty miles ahead of her at 0230 hours, barring her passage into the Atlantic. However, if he now turned north towards *Bismarck* he could hope to meet the German squadron at about 0200 hours with every possible advantage. The German ships would be silhouetted against the afterglow of sunset and the British would be in darkness. It was in this modern age the equivalent of having the wind-gauge.

After action stations had been ordered on *Hood* and *Prince of Wales*, therefore, Admiral Holland altered course. They would turn to starboard and heading in a more northerly direction, they would prepare to meet the *Bismarck* any time after 0140 hours. *Hood* and *Prince of Wales* would fire at *Bismarck* while *Suffolk* and *Norfolk* were supposed to attack *Prinz Eugen*.

But when after an hour and a half there was no further word from *Suffolk*, Holland realized that the cruiser had lost the Germans. So he swung around and headed southwards on the course last known to have been followed by *Bismarck*. The destroyers continued northwards, and missed the Germans. It had all worked precisely as Admiral Holland had calculated. At 0141 the destroyers on the old course were passing just ten miles south of the German ships. Only the nastiness of the weather prevented *Bismarck* from being spotted right there.

Just before 0300, *Suffolk* piped up once more: she had made contact with the *Bismarck*, which was now – according to the plot made hastily in the bridge of *Hood* – about thirty-five miles northwest. They were on a line almost along the southern coast of Iceland. *Bismarck* was just about to break out into the Atlantic.

Hood and *Prince of Wales* changed course and swung north to intercept. On *Bismarck*, Admiral Lütjens continued his steady course southwest heading for the Atlantic. He still did not know that the British capital ships were out this night.

The course alterations had changed the odds of battle remarkably. For if they had met on the old course, it would have been head-to-beam and the British ships would have had the advantage of a larger beam target while the Germans would have been firing at the bows of the British ships.

But now by overhauling the Germans from the rear, the British would have to come up at a wide angle instead of a narrow one, and there would be a long period when the *Hood*'s beam would be exposed. It had been very unlucky that *Suffolk* had lost track of *Bismarck* at that critical juncture.

At 0400 hours *Hood*'s men had been at action stations for four long hours. On the bridge it was estimated that the Germans were twenty miles away, and an hour later fifteen miles away.

At 0510 hours Admiral Holland signalled his ships to be ready for action at a moment's notice. Aboard *Hood* and *Prince of Wales* the captains broadcast to their crews. It was about to begin.

18

Sudden Death

It was 0035 hours, the day had just dawned, and *Hood* and *Prince of Wales* were steaming southwest at 28 knots. A vessel could be seen just coming up on the horizon. It was *Bismarck*, and she was seventeen miles away. *Prinz Eugen* could be seen ahead of her.

Two minutes later the blue pendant went up and together *Hood* and *Prince of Wales* turned to starboard towards the enemy. Eight minutes later the admiral ordered the ships to turn again and to prepare to engage *Prinz Eugen* which was to the left of *Bismarck*. Moments later he changed his mind and designated *Bismarck* as the target.

On board *Bismarck* the last hours had been particularly anxious. A signal from German headquarters late on the night of the twenty-third had indicated that there was still no activity on the part of the big British ships. At about 0200 hours an aircraft alarm was sounded on *Bismarck* and a Catalina flying boat appeared overhead. It was one of several sent out from Iceland to find the Germans, but the ships were lost from view by the colour of the sea in darkness and the plane soon disappeared.

At 0300 hours *Prinz Eugen* heard *Suffolk* for the first time in three hours and passed along the message. Then nothing. At 0500 hours the listening-post reported hearing the sounds of two fast-moving ships approaching on the port bow, but the look-outs saw nothing until the third gunnery officer eventually spotted smoke in the southeast. The alarm bells rang out and as the two ships moved closer one of them was identified as *Hood*.

At 0552 hours the range was 25,000 yards. On *Hood*'s bridge it was being called out as the chief yeoman of signals stood by waiting on the admiral's order. When it came he hoisted the signal JD – open fire.

'Open Fire,' said Captain Kerr. 'Shoot,' said the gunnery officer in the control tower.

On board *Bismarck* Admiral Lütjens was making the same preparations, except that his ship's guns were loaded with high explosive shells with impact fuses. The Germans had thought all along that the ships they saw were cruisers. Before the firing began only a handful, not including Lütjens, realized that these were capital ships.

The flash and the sound of the British guns came to the Germans across the water. They had to wait for the shells to fall, but when they did the first salvo from *Hood* fell near *Prinz Eugen* and it was not dangerously close. *Prince of Wales*'s first shots were 1,000 yards short of *Bismarck*.

The German shooting was better. The first salvo fell ahead of *Hood*. The second salvo from *Bismarck* fell astern of her. The third came closer and a curtain of splashes separated her from *Prince of Wales*.

The British were having difficulty. There was no doubt about that. The Germans had achieved the old weather gauge. The British ships were steaming into the wind and the lenses of the range-finders on the forward turrets were drenched, especially those on *Hood*. By keeping *Prince of Wales* very close to him Admiral Holland had made it easy for the Germans to find the range. Furthermore, the angle of approach had been such that instead of giving the Germans a narrow target he had given them a very broad one.

There was then the question of guns. The angle of fire was such that *Hood* and *Prince of Wales* could bring only ten

guns to bear on the enemy. After the first salvo one gun on
Prince of Wales failed and that meant nine to the German's
eight. In addition to this the British were firing at both
Prinz Eugen and *Bismarck*, while the Germans were firing
only at *Hood*.

The Germans, in other words, had all the best of it.
Luck and the reaction of their admiral gave them the
advantage.

They were also firing very well. *Prinz Eugen*'s second
salvo had straddled the *Hood* and started a fire on the boat-
deck amidships. It was a deep, red glow of flame before
thick smoke began to pour out of whatever was burning.
It was 0555 hours and only three minutes had gone by.

It was burning cordite. That much was certain because
Midshipman Dundas, who had joined the ship just five
months earlier, heard it reported. He was midshipman of
the watch on the upper bridge, but because the bridge was
closed in he himself could not see aft. But the torpedo
officer, who was at the starboard after end of the bridge,
reported to the captain that a cordite fire had broken out
on the starboard side of the boat deck. That was why it was
burning so hotly and the flames were so real.

Seaman Robert Tilburn was sheltering underneath the
forward bridge on the port side of *Hood* just in front of the
forward 4-inch gun mounting. He saw the fire and reckoned
it came from an ammunition locker for 4-inch shells. Soon
the guns, which were loaded, began firing.

From the bridge came the order to the damage control
parties to put the fire out. Almost immediately ammunition
started exploding. It was too dangerous for anyone to
approach the fire.

To Tilburn the popping of the ammunition sounded
like Chinese fire-crackers. Petty Officer Bishop, gunner's
mate in charge of the guns, ordered everyone to stand clear.
Up forward A and B turrets were firing all the while.

Ordinary Signalman Albert Edward Briggs was stationed on *Hood*'s compass platform and he saw the opening of the action. He also overheard Admiral Holland talking to Captain Kerr. The admiral remarked that *Prinz Eugen* had turned away and that *Bismarck* seemed to be turning away as *Hood* was firing. The admiral ordered *Hood* to turn 40° to starboard, so that *Bismarck* would be ahead of them again. They closed to twelve miles.

Hood fired again. On the bridge they thought they had hit *Bismarck* squarely. Then came the fire in the ready-use lockers of the 4-inch guns.

'She has hit us on the boat deck,' reported the squadron gunnery officer.

'Leave it until the ammunition is gone,' was Admiral Holland's reply.

The Captain then picked up the telephone to ring the spotting top. He could not get through.

Hood turned to port. The move was designed to bring the after turrets to bear on the enemy. Just then *Bismarck* fired a broadside, and in a few seconds *Hood* was hidden by the curtain of shell splashes.

A column of flame shot up from *Hood*'s centre section. One witness said it was four times the height of the mainmast, a long, pale red tongue reaching for the sky.

On the bridge Midshipman Dundas was thrown off his feet with everyone else up there. But there was no noise as Dundas picked himself up and looked over the side. He saw a mass of brown smoke drifting along the port side. The ship was listing to port, and the list was growing. He climbed uphill along what had once been a level deck and scrambled to one of the windows to escape. The officer of the watch was climbing through another window.

Seaman Tilburn felt the ship shake. Then she tilted and a lot of debris and bodies began to rain down on the decks. She started going down at the stern and Tilburn struggled up on to the forecastle because his old perch was now under water. He took off his gas-mask and coat. Water from the forecastle washed over him and sent him over the side.

Three others were with him. One was killed by something in the explosion, another was hit in the stomach and the third simply disappeared. It was dead silent. There was no noise at all.

As he went over the side, it was eerie. There was absolutely no one else around. On the compass platform, Signalman Briggs had seen the explosion, too.

'The compass is gone,' said the officer of the watch to the admiral. 'Then move her over to after control,' replied Admiral Holland. Already she had started to list. As the admiral spoke she lurched to port, and she was over at 25°.

Briggs saw others, officers and men, scramble to get off the bridge. Only the admiral stood there, not moving at all.

Briggs got out of the starboard window. The navigator and the squadron gunnery officer were there with him. He was through the door and by this time the water was level with the compass platform. Then everything went black. In what seemed like a moment he found himself on the surface of the water. The bows of *Hood* were standing vertical to the sea. He was looking at the bottom of his ship.

What had happened, as they reconstructed it later, was that one of *Bismarck*'s shells had penetrated straight down through those never-strengthened decks until it went below the waterline and exploded in the 4-inch magazine, which in turn blew up the 15-inch after magazine. That had caused the column of flame.

Seaman Tilburn looked up as he swam away. Then the mast struck him and the ship fell over on top of him. He was caught by the legs, but he managed to cut off his sea-boots as he was being dragged down. When he surfaced the bows were just sticking out of the water. Moments later she sank.

Aboard *Bismarck* they saw her blow up and break in two. Just before she fell apart, the guns of A and B turrets fired one more blast. Then she went down.

On board *Prince of Wales* they watched in horror, and then Captain Leach turned hard to starboard to avoid the wreckage, as more than 1,400 men went down to their deaths.

The battle was unequal now and the guns of *Prince of Wales* were hardly in shape to continue the fight. But fight she did until it became apparent that if she continued she also might be sunk. At 0613 hours she turned away. It was twenty-one minutes after Admiral Holland had led the two ships into battle.

The signal was flashed from Admiral Wake-Walker in *Norfolk*. '*Hood* has blown up,' it said.

In London, and all through the fleet wherever the ships and men were, the news was stunning. Mighty *Hood* was dead.

Epilogue

When *Prince of Wales* turned away from the battle zone badly damaged she headed southeast. On *Bismarck* Admiral Lütjens was pleased to break off the action and get out into the Atlantic.

Bismarck had been hit three times. The most serious damage was a hole in her oil storage tanks so that she was losing a large quantity of fuel. *Prinz Eugen* had not been hit, but Lütjens was eager not to tangle with any more British warships. So he headed for the coast of France to repair *Bismarck* before continuing his mission.

Bismarck limped out of the battle zone leaving only the flotsam and jetsam of *Hood* bobbing up and down in the cold sea.

Admiral Wake-Walker, now senior officer, ordered *Hood*'s destroyers to the battle zone to pick up survivors. Planes which had been flying in the area and had watched the battle gave the co-ordinates. The destroyers, four of them, came hurrying along, and as they sped to the rescue of their comrades, blankets, medicines, food and clean clothing were prepared.

The destroyers moved down in a line abreast of each other, so that one of them could spot survivors and could then pass the word to the others.

They steamed for two long hours. HMS *Electra* finally reached the precise spot of the battle. Her captain and her officers could not believe what they saw. All they found were patches of oil on the water, a floating drawer, a few unrecognizable bits of wood and three Carley rafts.

Midshipman Dundas was on one raft, Seaman Tilburn was on the second and Signalman Briggs was on the third. That was all. Absolutely, irrevocably all.

The shock was so great, the aura of disbelief so tremendous, that they searched, turned and searched again, unable to believe it. For *Hood* was not just *another* ship of the fleet, but a command vessel that had a mystique all its own. She was *the* ship, *the* symbol of the Royal Navy's might. She had been all through the twenties, the thirties and into the forties, even though times had changed. That was it. As this tragedy so clearly proved, modern warfare had passed her by.

The evidence was before their eyes. They found a marine's hat, a few small pieces of wreckage and nothing else, absolutely nothing else.

The three survivors were taken aboard *Electra*. When they had recovered sufficiently from the exposure and the shock they told their stories. These bore out entirely the dreadful vision of nothingness that their rescuers had witnessed.

The destroyers turned north for Iceland to refuel.

In London the news was greeted with the same sense of deep shock. There was no sense in trying to deny it. German radio was broadcasting triumphantly the news of the sinking of Britain's mightiest battle-cruiser. So the news was released to the BBC and the newspapers. It was several days before the world seemed sane again. Only revenge, the wiping out of *Bismarck* could accomplish this, and it did. But that is another tale. . . .

Bibliographical Note

The research for this book was done largely at the Public Records Office in London in the summer of 1975. I am indebted to a number of people there for unfailing courtesy and understanding of a researcher's problems.

I also wish to thank the archivists at the Imperial War Museum for much assistance, and the librarians at the British Museum and the Naval Museum at Greenwich.

Lt Cdr (Ret.) C. McD. Stuart of the Naval Library in London was most helpful.

Among the books consulted were:

The Mighty Hood by Ernle Bradford, which deals with the ship from a very different vantage point than my own

Pursuit by Ludovic Kennedy, which tells much of the story of the great tragic battle in which *Hood* went down

Running a Big Ship, or *Ten Commandments* by Rory O'Conor, commander of the *Hood*, 1933-6

Cunningham, the Commander by S. W. C. Pack

The War At Sea, Vol. 1 by Capt. S. W. Roskill

A Sailor's Odyssey by Viscount Cunningham of Hyndhope

The War At Sea by John Winton

Das Geheimnis der Bismarck by Fritz Otto Busch

The Bismarck Episode by Russell Grenfell

The British Navies in the Second World War by Wilbur James

Cruise of the Bismarck by F. E. McMurtrie

HMS Hood by Lt Stanley Geary RNVR

One Year of Life (the story of HMS *Prince of Wales*) by Alan and Gordon Franklin

La Tragique Odysée du Cuirasse 'Bismarck' by Jean Trogoff

Great Britain and the German Navy by E. L. Woodward

HMS Hood, a Short Account of her Forebears and Herself prepared for Hiarns and Miller, naval printers

Schlachtschiff Bismarck by Jochen Brennecke, US Naval Institute

Exploits and End of the Battleship Bismarck by Capt. Gerhard Bidlingmaier, US Naval Institute Proceedings, July 1958

At the Public Records Office some of the valuable documents were The Supplement to the London *Gazette*, 16 October 1947

The Admiralty records on the sinking of the *Bismarck*

The report of proceedings of the Board of Inquiry into the loss of HMS *Hood*

The Admiralty reports on the activities of *Hood*'s marines and naval force in Norway

The logs of *Hood*, and the war diaries, and various reports of the Battle Squadron from 1921 to 1941

Index

	DATE DUE		
70	FEB 24 '81		
1523	Mar 31 81		
2	Mar 31 '81		
4/4.9	R 28 '81		
5285	SEP 10 '81		
1462	JUL 22 '82		
SC3	OCT 18 84		
APR 25 85	2650		
2410	JUL 16 87		

359.3
Hoy

Hoyt, Edwin P

Sunk by the B........